THE ULTIMATE GUIDE
TO ELK HUNTING

Books by Bob Robb

Hunting Wild Boar in California
Elk Hunting with the Experts
Deer Hunting Coast to Coast (with Craig Boddington)
The Field & Stream Guide to Bowhunting
Bowhunting Essentials
Elk Essentials
Black Bear Essentials
Mule Deer—North American Challenge

THE ULTIMATE GUIDE TO ELK HUNTING

Techniques and Strategies of North
America's Greatest Elk Hunters

BOB ROBB AND GERALD BETHGE

THE LYONS PRESS

Guilford, Connecticut
An imprint of The Globe Pequot Press

Printed in the United States of America

10 9 8 7 6 5 4 3

Library of Congress Cataloging-in-Publication Data
Robb, Bob.
    Ultimate guide to elk hunting / by Bob Robb and Gerald Bethge.
        p. cm.
    ISBN 1-58574-180-9
    1. Elk hunting. I. Title.
    SK303 .R633 2000
    799.2'76542—dc21

                                                            00-64170

CONTENTS

INTRODUCTION

E lk have long captured the imagination and spirit of adventurers like Lewis and Clark and sport hunters as far back as Teddy Roosevelt. They have remained in the mind's eye of most big game hunters for decades since. And why not? Elk are big and powerful animals that present sportsmen with the ultimate hunting challenge and experience. Often inhabiting some of the most scenic territory, elk are synonymous with wilderness. Any hunter who has ever heard the eerie beckoning of a mature, lovesick bull bugling for a cow's attention will readily attest to that. A mature bull elk's bugle is absolute testament to its wildness.

No matter where one stalks elk, the first lesson learned is that they are not easy animals to hunt. Despite its huge body and antler size, a big bull—looking to shake off a hunter on his back trail—can disappear faster than Houdini.

In the 30 years I have hunted elk, I have witnessed firsthand mature 6×6 bulls enter black timber and, within seconds, never be seen or heard from again. I have seen bulls stand at the edge of cover totally motionless for what seemed like hours before feeling safe enough to leave cover and enter an open park. I have jumped elk and seen them burst from the most unlikely cover—a single patch of scrub oak which didn't seem large enough to hide a deer, never mind an elk. From the wild, pristine country they inhabit to their cunning ability to elude danger, elk continually prove to be superior game animals.

Hunters who challenge elk soon understand they have to learn all they can to be consistently successful at taking big bulls. No matter which of the huntable North American subspecies you'll pursue, whether it's the Rocky Mountain elk, Roosevelt elk, or Manitoba elk, you'll need honed skills and knowledge to take the challenge on equal ground. Over the years, I have read every book available by all the pros who stalk elk. I can tell you this with confidence, Bob Robb's knowledge and experience of hunting elk is second to none!

Robb is an avid outdoorsman. His hunting articles have appeared in all of the major outdoor publications for nearly thirty years. An accomplished hunter with gun or bow, his big game adventures have lured him to places across the globe. Robb has hunted elk in every state, Canadian province, and even in his own backyard—the wilds of Alaska.

Gerry Bethge has been my friend for twenty years. He is a dedicated and versatile big-game hunter. Bethge has been an editor of several major outdoor publications, including *Outdoor Life*. He has published stories written by elk hunting authorities for more than twenty-five years. In fact, he has probably read and absorbed more about elk and elk hunting than anyone I know. Like Bob Robb, he has also hunted elk extensively, across North America. Put Bethge together with Robb, and you've got an unbeatable elk hunting team—who enthusiastically share all their combined elk hunting information unselfishly, as well as tactics from many other elk hunting experts, within the pages of this book.

If I had to share a camp with just one seasoned elk-hunting companion, it would be Bob Robb. He is by far one of the most respected and accomplished hunters today. Along with Bethge, he shares his elk hunting wisdom, experience, and tactics within the pages of this book. The information will become your bible to successful elk hunting. It's mine.

—*Peter Fiduccia*
Editor-in-Chief
Outdoorsman's Edge Book Club

1

NORTH AMERICAN ELK: WHAT ARE THEY?

When I think of the Rocky Mountain West, I envision many things. Tall mountain peaks, awesome in their size and beauty, define the portrait. Large stands of uncut timber, lush meadows of tall grass, crystal-clear streams and rivers, and emeraldlike lakes dot the landscape. Breathtaking sunrises and sunsets color a cobalt-blue sky at dawn and dusk with variations of reds, oranges, and purples that no mortal artist could ever create.

Wildlife is a large part of my picture. When I dream back to all the days I've spent climbing the mountains of the West, the days spent without viewing wildlife are those most empty. Big game like deer and bears and mountain lions define the region for me. Small game and a variety of birds are prominent in the picture, too, providing amusement whenever they appear.

But no creature defines the West like a big bull elk.

What sportsman in North America has not dreamed of following in the footsteps of Lewis and Clark, going West and hunting elk? For the big-game hunter of today, no animal creates excitement and stimulates dreams like the magnificent mature bull elk.

Elk have so many things going for them. The country in which they live is beyond compare, not only in North America but the world. They are big, powerful animals, with large bodies and large antlers. Their meat is some of the most delicious and nutritious in all of nature. Despite their gregarious, family-oriented disposition, elk are secretive, especially when pressured by people. Filling an elk tag is no easy task. They are the ultimate challenge for those who hunt members of the North American deer family.

No big game animal symbolizes the West, and what it stands for, like a bull elk. They are the stuff that sportsmen's dreams are made of.

There are lots of elk in North America today—more than a million, at last count, more so than at any time since the turn of the century. The future of elk, and elk hunting, is bright. As we step into the 21st century, it can be rightfully said that the good old days of elk hunting are right now.

The history of elk, like that of all animal species prior to the advent of modern census methods, is somewhat cloudy. It is believed that North America was home to some 10 million elk prior to the arrival of the first European explorers. Sir Francis Drake and his crew are thought to have been the first Europeans to actually see elk on the continent, glimpsing what they called "a very large and fat Deere" in the inland regions of California in the summer of 1579. These "Deere" are believed to have been Tule elk, which Drake and his men saw "by the thousands."

The first settlers along the East Coast of North America also saw elk, which at that time could be found in good numbers across the continent. For example, in 1670 one John Lederer described seeing "Red Deer" (elk) along the Chesapeake Bay. Other accounts by early white settlers have elk living from New England as far south as the settlements went.

In fact, during the Pleistocene Epoch there were 10 subspecies of *Cervus* in North America. Of these, six are extinct today. They are the Eastern elk (*C. canadensis canadensis*); Merriam elk (*C. canadensis merriami*); a fossil elk found in Wisconsin (*C. whitneyi Allen*); a fossil elk from New Mexico (*C. lascrucensis Frick*); a southern California fossil elk (*C. aguangae Frick*); and an unknown fossil subspecies from Alaska (Murie, 1951). A reclassification of *Cervus* in 1973 changed the familiar species name of elk from *canadensis* to the European form, *elaphus*; this is how elk subspecies are referred to by modern scientists.

Tales from pioneer times are filled with accounts of the abundant wildlife living across the vast expanses of the continent. Reports of elk are prominent in many of these stories. The journals of Lewis and Clark document the pair's legendary expedition across North America from 1804 to 1806 and are the first extensive documentation of the animals of the West. In those journals are more than 600 references to elk, which were abundant and used by natives for food, leather, and assorted bone products.

From those estimated 10 million North American elk prior to the white man's arrival, elk numbers had dwindled to fewer than 100,000 by 1907, with populations continuing to decline. The advance of modern man and civilization drove the elk and other wildlife off their traditional habitat, while commercial hunting for both meat and hides decimated game numbers across the country. In 1922, it is believed that only 92,000 elk remained, of which a lit-

An estimated 10,000,000 elk lived in North America prior to the white man's arrival. After a plunge to only 92,000 animals in 1922, populations have rebounded and are now estimated to be near 1 million today.

tle over 37,000 lived in Yellowstone National Park, the Teton National Forest, and parts of Canada. Many people believe that without the creation of Yellowstone National Park, Wyoming; Olympic National Park, Washington; and a private California reserve specifically set aside for Tule elk, the possibility of any elk remaining alive in the wild today would be remote.

The picture today is so different from the one painted in the early 1900s it is astounding, like comparing a color television with a black and white set. By the late 1970s more than 500,000 elk populated North America. Today, that number stands at an estimated 1 million, a population boom that boggles the mind. The increase is due in no small measure to the efforts of dedicated sports hunters and hunting-related conservation organizations such as the Rocky Mountain Elk Foundation, both of which have raised astonishing sums of money and donated countless hours of time working in conjunction with state wildlife managers. With a few exceptions, biologists are predicting that there will be even more elk across the continent as time goes by.

The story of elk in Colorado, which has the highest elk population of any state or Canadian province, is illustrative of what has occurred throughout the West. At the beginning of the 20th century, the Colorado Division of Wildlife estimates there were fewer than 2000 elk remaining statewide. Intensive management, transplants from other states, and the closing of the hunting season for 26 years in the early part of the century all led to a steady, rapid rise in elk numbers. By the spring of 2000, Colorado reported that its elk herd had expanded to some 265,000 animals. It had grown so large so fast that it had exceeded population objectives in most areas of the state; a record-number 106,000 antlerless and either-sex hunting licenses were issued for the fall 2000 season in an attempt to get the burgeoning elk herd back under control.

SUBSPECIES

Today there are four subspecies of North American elk roaming the continent. They are:

Rocky Mountain Elk (*Cervus elaphus nelsoni*): The most numerous subspecies, they can be found in the central to northern Rocky Mountains, including eastern British Columbia, most of Alberta, and northern Saskatchewan. They may also be found in eastern Oregon and eastern Washington, Idaho, Montana, Colorado, Utah, Nevada, New Mexico, Arizona, and parts of California. Transplants have seen *nelsoni* introduced into states as diverse as Pennsylvania, Virginia, Michigan, Oklahoma, Texas, Kansas, and the Dakotas, as well as parts of eastern Canada.

Roosevelt Elk (*Cervus elaphus roosevelti*): The largest-bodied elk can be found in the dense rain forests of the Pacific Northwest, from northern California up through Oregon, Washington, the British Columbia mainland and Vancouver Island, Afognak and Raspberry Islands, Alaska, as well as near Ketchikan, Alaska.

Manitoba Elk (*Cervus elaphus manitobensis*): The second-largest-bodied of all our elk, they are located in pockets of southwestern Manitoba, southern Saskatchewan, and southeastern Alberta.

Tule Elk (*Cervus elaphus nannodes*): Our smallest elk, they live only in various locations throughout California. These splay-hoofed marsh dwellers numbered an estimated 500,000 animals before the mid-1800s. By the middle of the 19th century, their numbers had dropped to exactly eight animals. Today they number nearly 2500.

Tule elk, our smallest subspecies, live only in parts of California. After the population dropped to only eight elk in the mid-19th century, there are nearly 2500 animals today.

Elk are the second largest member of the North American deer family, surpassed in both body size and antler mass only by the moose (*Alces alces*). The largest of the four subspecies is the Roosevelt elk. Mature Roosevelt bulls weigh between 700 and 1100 pounds, though some Roosevelts living on Alaska's Afognak and Raspberry islands can weigh nearly 1300 pounds. Records show some Afognak Island elk at having field dressed at nearly 1000 pounds. Cows are smaller, weighing between 575 and 625 pounds.

The Manitoba elk is the next largest subspecies, with mature bulls weighing an average of nearly 800 pounds, and cows 600 pounds. A mature Rocky Mountain elk bull averages 700 pounds on the hoof, with cows weighing an average of 525 pounds. Tule elk are the smallest subspecies, with bulls weighing an average of 400 pounds, cows an average of 325 pounds.

Take a close look, and you'll notice that elk have no useful teeth in the front portion of their upper jaw, wearing instead a dental pad over their lower front teeth. Elk have a total of 32 teeth, including the "ivories" so prized by hunters. These are not real ivory, but incisiform canine teeth. Also known as "whistlers," "buglers," and "elk teeth," these two teeth are located in the forward part of the upper jaw.

Distinctive antlers are the most intriguing attribute of the bull elk. Large sets of trophy-class antlers are what all elk hunters dream about, and are hard-earned prizes to be proud of.

The main beams of a mature Rocky Mountain bull elk's antler average between 40 and 60 inches in length, with six distinct tines, or points. They can weigh up to 30 pounds per set.

A mature Rocky Mountain bull elk antler usually consists of a single long main beam between 40 and 60 inches in length that sweeps up and back and has six distinct tines, or points (nontypical points are possible as well). The first two tines are called the brow and bez tines, and grow close together at the base of the skull, sweeping outward over the elk's face. The third, or trez, tine begins farther up the beam, and usually angles forward. The "royal" point, as the fourth point is called, is generally the longest point of all, usually the dominant tine of the rack. The remaining points are formed by a fork at the rear of the main beam. This conformation is typical of the Manitoba subspecies as well.

The only difference between the antlers of the above two subspecies and those of the Roosevelt and Tule elk subspecies is the "crowning" at the end of the main beam on many of these latter bulls. Here, instead of a simple fork as in the case of Rocky Mountain and Manitoba elk, the antlers sometimes, but not always, form a cluster of points, much like that which the red stag of Europe and New Zealand wears. These crown points can give these bulls a total of seven to nine points per side. A pair of elk antlers from a mature bull of all species of elk save the diminutive Tule elk generally weighs between 20 and 30 pounds.

Historically, elk played a large part in the development of North America. Native Americans utilized them widely, eating their lean, nutritious meat, tanning their hides and using them for robes, moccasins, and shelter, and making after-products from bones, fat, hooves, teeth, and internal organs. In the modern West, elk continue to play a large role in shaping the future. Contemporary land management planning often revolves around its effects on wildlife, and with elk numbers expanding throughout the region, these regal animals are always in the minds of present-day planners.

Just knowing there are elk out there with me as I hike through the West makes me feel content. They are noble, fascinating animals, worthy of our respect, admiration, and protection. Having the privilege to hunt them each fall is one of my most treasured adventures. Once you hunt them, it will be very difficult for you to escape the magic of "elk fever." I know. I haven't missed an elk season since 1977.

2

BASIC
ELK
BEHAVIOR

To successfully hunt any species of big game, it is imperative to understand the animal's habits and haunts, its likes and dislikes, and how it will react to hunting pressure. After all, you can't shoot an elk if you can't find one. With little or no knowledge of the animal itself, you may as well be buying a lottery ticket as an elk tag; the chances of locating a bull will be that low. However, the more you learn about elk, where they live during the various seasons, what their wants and needs are, and how they will act during "odd" periods—a hot spell during late fall, for example—the better your chances of finding them.

As you learn more about elk, you'll find that new questions keep popping up. Your curiosity will be tickled; you'll want to learn even more. The more time you spend in elk country, the more fascinating it becomes. It's a magical world, and you'll soon come to realize that there really are no set, definitive answers to any of the questions you've been asking all these years. Just when you think you have the game all figured out, the elk will throw you a curve, and you'll strike out once again.

That's the wonder of elk, and of elk hunting.

To give you some idea of how elk spend their days, here's a brief rundown of a year in the life of an elk.

A YEAR IN THE LIFE

Summer is a magical time in the mountains of the West. Spring flowers brighten the landscape, temperatures are mild, and the grass is lush and full of high-quality nutrients.

Elk calves are born in summer, usually early June, after being carried by the cow for 8 to 8½ months. Most elk have only one calf

Cow elk drop their calves in June after a gestation period of 8 to 8½ months. Calving grounds are in areas where there's lots of feed, plus all-important escape cover.

per year, with twins a rarity. Calf elk weigh around 25 to 30 pounds at birth. Calving grounds are located in the upper reaches of the elk's winter range, where there is plenty of water and lots of grassy meadows bordered by dark escape-cover timber. The tannish calves blend in well with the surrounding countryside when they lie immobile, flattened against the ground. They instinctively hide in this manner when they perceive danger, more like forest-dwelling animals than the open-country ruminants that modern elk have evolved into.

For the first two to four weeks after birth, cows and their newborns stay away from the herd while each mother tends to her calf as it gets its walking legs. After that the cows, calves, and very young bulls herd up, with numbers often reaching into the hundreds. Herd members look out for each other, with some cows actually acting as baby-sitters when other cows with calves go off to feed.

During this time, bull elk are a lot like stereotypical men who would rather be playing poker with the boys than sitting around the house listening to a women's tea party. The mature bulls are off by themselves now. They congregate in small bachelor herds numbering between two and eight animals. They like to move to high elevations, where they can rest and put on weight, with cooling afternoon breezes warding off flies, mosquitoes, and other insects.

The bulls begin antler growth anytime between January and June, depending upon their age, testosterone level, and the photoperiod (the amount of daylight on a given day of the year). The youngest bulls start antler growth last because their antlers are the smallest. Bulls expend as much energy growing new antlers as pregnant cows do growing new calves.

The pedicles, or antler bases, start growing faster in May and June, thanks to a boost in testosterone levels. In yearling bulls, antler growth does not begin until June or July and ends in August or September, when the velvet is finally shed. In two-year-olds, the antlers

Bulls begin antler growth sometime between January and June. Antlers grow on pedicles, which accelerate their growth in May and June with a boost in testosterone levels.

begin growing in late April or early May, with velvet shed roughly in mid- to late August, a period of approximately 115 days. In three- and four-year-old bulls, antler growth begins sometime between mid-February and mid-March, with velvet being shed in early August. The growth of their antlers takes approximately 140 days. Mature bulls in the prime of life begin their antler growth earlier, between mid-January and late February. They shed their velvet in late July or early August, after a growth period of approximately 150 days.

As summer continues, elk put on lots of weight and live the good life. Cows and calves feed heavily and redefine the herd's pecking order and social structure. The bulls also feed heavily on lush grasses, their energy going not toward the raising of the young but to antler growth. Elk spend about 90 percent of their day feeding and resting, the other 10 percent in idle movement. They are very much like cattle in that about three-fourths of their resting time is used in bedding, while three-fourths of bedding time is used in ruminating.

As the days of August pass, most mature bulls have completed their antler growth. Testosterone levels are rising, and the breeding urge is getting stronger. The bulls now begin "raking" small trees, brush, and shrubs, both to strip their newly grown antlers of velvet and as a form of mock battle. They also begin sparring with each other, testing their strength as they prepare for the rut.

During the rut, elk stage mock battles with small trees and brush, often leaving vertical scars in the trunks of small trees with their sharp antler tines.

The rut begins in August, and is characterized by sparring between bulls of similar size and age. Latitude, local climatic conditions, and photoperiod control the actual rut timing.

The timing of the breeding period varies, and depends upon several factors. These include local climactic conditions and the condition of the animals. Generally speaking, elk rut earlier in the southern latitudes and later in the northern latitudes. Scientists believe this is due to the importance of elk calves being dropped in the spring when the weather is mild and the dangerous winter cold and snows are gone and no longer a threat to calf survival. For example, you'll normally find elk rutting heavily in Arizona and New Mexico in August, when the bulls in more northern climes like Montana are just getting under way. Tule elk in California's hot Owens Valley have been known to begin rutting in late July and early August, even before their velvet has been totally shed.

As the bulls become ready for the rut, the bugling and forming of the harems begin. Cows are beginning to come into heat, and the bulls begin competing for the right to breed them. Young bulls are driven from the cow-calf groups as the older, more mature bulls move in to try to dominate the breeding cycle.

The younger, "yearling" spike bulls don't vanish completely. At 15 months of age, they are sexually mature and could breed a cow. They rarely do, however. More often than not they can be found in small bachelor groups of up to 15 animals, acting as if they're not quite sure what to do. But the smaller, two- and three-year-old bulls have strong breeding urges, and though they cannot compete with the larger herd bulls in a face-to-face fight, they often hang around the fringes of the herd, hoping to breed a cow when the opportunity presents itself. Often called "satellite" bulls because they spend so much time orbiting the herd, these younger bulls are often the animals that hunters call into range.

It should be remembered that while the bulls are strutting around acting like kings during the rutting cycle, it is really the older cows that are the true leaders of the herd. The lead, or herd, cow is the animal that takes responsibility for the day-to-day life of the group, leading it to food, water, and bedding sites, giving off the alarm bark when danger approaches, and leading the herd off when danger is perceived. As an elk hunter, no matter the season, you must be constantly on the lookout for these herd cows. Nine times out of 10, they're the ones that will ruin a stalk for you.

Generally speaking, the rutting cycle lasts through mid-October, though it peaks in early to mid-September, and some breeding may actually occur into November. The rut is hard on bulls. They may lose as much as 40 percent of their total body weight and leave the rut very much weakened. Now the bigger bulls just seem to vanish from the face of the earth.

Where do they go? The bigger bulls that have completed their part of the rut will head for areas where they will not be disturbed by man or beast. They need peace and quiet so they can rest and regain their strength to combat the rigors of the coming winter. Many of these big bulls go off by themselves, though sometimes they'll go off in pairs or threes, and sometimes they'll have a younger satellite-type bull or two with them. These bulls often dive off into the dark timber, rugged areas that are difficult for people to access, the ground covered with thick brush, blowdowns, and steep cuts, and highlighted by thick stands of mature softwoods. Here they can rest and regain some strength before they go on feeding binges as they try to put on enough weight in the form of body fat to help them through the coming winter.

As the calendar moves forward, elk continue to feed heavily in preparation for winter. When the snows and cold weather come, the animals start thinking about migrating down from their alpine summer and fall homes onto their winter range. This can begin anytime between late November and the end of December. Elk usually follow traditional migration routes from summer to winter range. However, most will not migrate down until the snows force them to. In years of light snowfall, the migration may be delayed by a few days, or even a few weeks. In years of heavy snows, the migration may begin a bit earlier than normal. Predicting the actual migration before winter weather sets in is akin to reading tarot cards and tea leaves.

A few of the older, stronger, prime bull elk may remain high in the mountains for an extended period of time. These old bachelors don't relish the thought of spending any more time with the women and children than they absolutely have to. Since they are not concerned with the raising of the young, they worry only about themselves. Their thick coats and layers of fat are tremendous insulators, keeping them warm well below 0°F. These bulls are able to find forage even in deep snow, and have been known to winter in areas where the snows are 4 feet deep or more. But, by and large, when winter comes elk head for the easier life of the winter range.

The elk are in a survival mode during winter months. They move little, trying to conserve their energy as best they can, traveling only to find new feed or to get out of strong winds and chill.

An elk's coat is a tremendous insulator, offering protection from all but the most bitter cold. Elk often bed right in the snow to stay warm.

When winter finally begins to break along about March, elk are restless. They know that as the high meadows are exposed from beneath the winter snows, lush, high-quality grasses and other forage will be available to them. By late March, the cows, calves, and younger bulls have usually begun their trek back along the traditional migration corridors to their summer range. The older, more mature bulls usually precede the other elk, their trek inhibited only by the snowline itself. Once on the summer range, the cows feed heavily in anticipation of the new calf crop, while the bulls feed and rest as their new antlers begin to grow.

DAILY MOVEMENT PATTERNS

Elk are restless animals, in no small part because of the large amount of food they must eat each day to survive. Their largest movements are, of course, the seasonal migrations between summer and winter range. However, once they have settled into a particular range, their daily movement patterns are dictated solely by the availability and quality of food, water, and protective cover. These movements are also affected by outside pressures, of which hunting is certainly no small factor.

Roosevelt elk movements tend to differ from those of their mountain cousins in that they travel shorter distances to have their needs met. These movements are often only related to altitude. For example, rather than head south for the winter, most Roosevelt elk must move only a relatively short distance to lower elevations to find the kind of food and cover they need in winter.

Generally speaking, elk begin their daily movements in late afternoon. From bedding areas in thick brush or timber, they begin feeding downhill toward meadows that contain lots of lush grasses on which they can feed. These meadows may be large, open parks, or they may be smaller meadows situated in little open pockets within the timber itself. Elk often reach these meadows just before dark.

The elk feed all night, alternating between resting and eating. Then, just before daylight, they herd up and begin their movement to their bedding areas up the slope. They reach these bedding areas by midmorning, where they once again spend the day resting and ruminating.

PREFERRED FOODS

Elk are herbivores, and concentrate on three main plant groups: browse, grasses, and forbs. And while little is known about elk and their preferences for certain foods at different times of the year, make no mistake about it: Elk prefer to eat fresh grasses whenever and wherever they can get them.

The amount of grass in an elk's diet depends upon where elk live and the availability of grass to eat. A 1973 study by R. C. Kufeld, titled *Foods Eaten by Rocky Mountain Elk*, states that Montana has a tremendous number of grassy meadows, and up to 84 percent of an elk's winter diet there is grass. In Idaho, that total drops to 65 percent. In areas where grass is less abundant, like Manitoba, Arizona, New Mexico, and Colorado, grass may make up as little as 22 percent of the total winter diet.

In summer, woody browse is prevalent, and thus becomes a more important part of the elk's diet. Aspen, currant, snowberry, serviceberry, huckleberry, bitterbrush, mountain mahogany, western juniper, peavine,

Elk crave the lush grasses found in open meadows and parks, but rarely can be found feeding there in daylight. This big old bull was an exception to the rule.

sagebrush, vetch, penstemon, and similar plants are all part of the elk's diet from time to time, depending on each plant's availability on a particular range. In New Mexico, the acorn nuts from scrub oak are eaten like candy when the elk can find them.

When studying an area you intend to hunt, try to learn what the preferred food sources are. Find out where they're located, and you're well on your way to finding the elk.

THE IMPORTANCE OF WATER

Elk need lots of water to drink, especially in the heat of summer and early fall. However, in most areas in which elk live, available water is not a problem. They will drink from anything and everything, including rivers, streams, ponds, lakes, seeps, and springs. Elk do prefer clean water to drink, though they will wallow in muddy water in summer and during the rut. The exception to the available-water theory is in the arid Southwest. Elk in Arizona have been known to travel miles each day to drink from the limited water sources there, which are often man-made stock tanks.

PROTECTIVE COVER

Undisturbed elk are not shy. They do not mind being out in the open, except in hot weather. Heat has a powerful effect on elk. Their thick, long-haired hides are tremendous insulators, which is a big reason

Elk need lots of water to drink, especially in hot weather. They'll also wallow in muddy pools and ponds to cool themselves off and to get rid of biting insects.

21

why elk prefer cool, shady cover, even in winter. In extremely cold conditions, when the temperature drops to $-30°F$ or more, elk often bed on open, sunny hillsides, trying to catch the warming rays of the sun. When it's hot, they often bed in or near snowbanks in spring and on into early summer. When there's no snow, they often bed in the dark timber, where the temperatures on the mountain are coolest. They also seek the shelter of the dark timber when winds are extremely strong and gusty.

When elk are pressured, as they are during the hunting seasons, they are not timid about taking to heavy cover and staying there. This is especially true of the larger bulls, who head for dark, leave-me-alone holes following the rut anyway. Herd cows—those wise old elk with many seasons under their belts and total control of herd movements—have been through several hunting seasons already. They know that when people begin invading the woods in fall, it's time to lead their charges away from the open meadows during daylight. They wisely choose to live their days in the cover of the timber, where few hunters come calling and even fewer have the skills to hunt quietly and effectively. That's why, even though you may find fresh tracks, droppings, and resting beds in the middle of large open meadows, you'll never see elk there. They visit only at night.

Nothing is ever set in concrete with elk. They can change their likes and dislikes as quickly as you can change your socks. The country and latitude in which they live, the available food, and water sources all affect their behavior. The challenge to you as an elk hunter is to understand elk needs and behavior in the area you hunt. In so doing, you will not only up your odds of filling your elk tag year in and year out, but you'll also have a greater appreciation for the elk themselves. That will lead directly to greater enjoyment of each day you spend in the woods.

And isn't that what elk hunting is all about?

3

MIND—
AND BODY—
OVER MATTER

You have to be tough to be a consistently successful elk hunter. Now that I have your attention, let me refine that statement a bit. Yes, you do have to be in good physical condition to successfully hunt elk. By the same token, you don't have to be a world-class marathon runner or triathlon champion to get the job done. But you do have to be able to hike around some of North America's most challenging terrain, at high altitudes, for several days without a lot of rest.

I made my first wilderness backpack hunt in 1968, at age 16. It remains my favorite way to hunt big game. Since then, I've learned two things: The mountains don't care that you're getting older, they're still steep and tough; and waiting until the week before opening day is too late to train your body for what lies ahead.

Just as important can be your mental conditioning. Elk hunting is hard work, and you can go days without a look at a good

Elk hunting is physically hard work. You must be in good physical condition to be able to hunt large drainages and steep mountains day after day in search of elk herds.

bull—or any elk at all. The weather might turn nasty, equipment may fail or get lost, and a steady diet of freeze-dried food can get old in a hurry. There are a million and one "gotchas" in elk hunting. I'm positive that Murphy, of Murphy's Law fame ("If something can go wrong, it will"), was an elk hunter. By themselves these little gremlins may mean nothing, but together they can make you as crazy as Jack Nicholson in *The Shining*. Elk hunters have to prepare themselves for the inevitable, and be able to keep smiling and hunting hard when all they really want to do is head for a home-cooked meal, a comfortable bed, and a clean pair of underwear.

MOUNTAIN SHAPE

Every year I speak with hundreds of prospective elk hunters. Many are from the Midwest and East, where the countryside is literally smaller in every sense of the word. When I describe what most elk country is like, they act as if they comprehend what I'm talking about. I tell them about steep mountains, deep canyons, high altitudes, and what it takes to be able to get around. Some of these prospective hunters have never met a meal they didn't like, nor have they ever been west of the Mississippi. They nod their heads as if they understand what I'm talking about, and when they say they'll be in good shape come elk season, I really think most of them believe it.

The truth of the matter is, the majority of elk hunters hit the woods each fall in good shape for a couch potato contest, not a week in the high country. It must be a combination of machismo and naivete that they actually believe they are in excellent condition and ready for the rigors of the peaks. Unless you've been elk hunting before, you really don't know how tough it can be.

You don't have to be a world-class athlete to hunt elk, but you should make a commitment to getting yourself into as good a physical condition as possible before hunting. All things being equal, hunters in good condition have a much better chance of bagging an elk than those in poor shape.

How so? By nature, elk are herd animals. Even in the best country, the herds are concentrated in a small part of the range. Hunters in good shape can cover more ground than those in poor condition, thereby upping their odds for locating the herds. Also, those in good shape can hunt more rugged parts of a given range, areas where the bulls like to go once the shooting starts. While fatigue can't be avoided on a week-long elk hunt, it affects those in top condition less. Just as important, those in good shape will simply enjoy their days in the woods more.

AEROBIC CONDITIONING

I was a multisport athlete in college, and have a bachelor's degree in physical education. For a time I designed training programs for high school and college athletes, as well as fitness programs for "weekend athletes." It was during this period that the importance of aerobic conditioning was impressed upon me.

Aerobic literally means "with oxygen." In elk hunting, your body will have to process lots of oxygen to function efficiently.

Altitude is one of the most underrated oxygen-stealers that elk hunters face. This is especially true for those who live in the low-elevation East and South. For example, the highest point of land in all of Pennsylvania is 3213 feet. The *lowest* point in all of Colorado is 3350 feet. With few exceptions, you'll be hunting western elk at a minimum elevation of 5000 feet. More than likely it will be between 7000 and 10,000 feet. Even well-conditioned low-elevation lungs have trouble straining oxygen from this thin high-country air.

The bottom line is, regardless of whether you hunt on your own or engage the services of an outfitter, you must prepare yourself physically to hunt elk. A strong pair of legs and lungs, plus a healthy heart, are the keys. Aerobic exercise will get you there.

Aerobic training directly benefits the most important muscle in your body—your heart. A proper aerobic exercise program will make the heart larger, stronger, and more efficient, enabling it to pump more blood with each beat. As your training program progresses, you'll find that your resting pulse rate will drop by a few

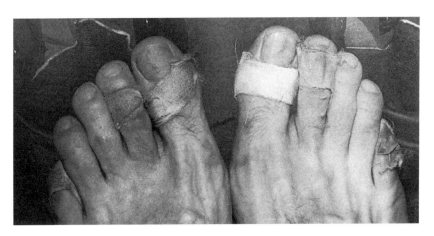

After a week of 12-mile-a-day hikes in the rugged Selway Wilderness Area of Idaho, my feet were shredded wheat. Be sure to toughen up your toes as well as your heart and lungs.

beats per minute. That's a sign that your heart is positively responding to your workouts.

The well-conditioned heart also recovers more quickly from stress. Picture yourself next elk season sprinting the last 100 yards to the top of a knoll, hoping to get a shot at the bull of your dreams before he disappears into the dark timber forever. If you're in shape, not only will you make it up the hill, but upon reaching the crest your heart rate will return to near-normal more quickly than if you are out of shape. That will certainly help you keep the crosshairs steady on your target.

Aerobic exercise benefits the body in other ways, too. It will decrease the amount of fat in your body, increase the number of capillaries in the circulatory system, and increase your lung capacity, all of which add up to making your body a leaner, more efficient machine. A well-conditioned body will be able to hunt harder and longer with less fatigue.

FOUR STEPS TO SUCCESS

1) Have a Medical Examination: If you haven't been exercising regularly, visit your doctor for a complete checkup. This is especially important if you're over 40 years of age. Once he gives the OK, you're ready to start.

2) Determine Your Target Heart Rate (THR): To gain maximum benefits from an aerobic exercise program you must maintain a sufficiently high heart rate during exercise. Your THR is the maximum rate your heart should be beating during exercise. To determine your THR, first subtract your age from 220, which will give you your predicted maximum heart rate (PMHR). For a 48-year-old like me, that's 172 beats per minute. Next, take 80 percent of your THR (for me, that's 138 beats per minute). To achieve a training effect, you must exceed your THR for a minimum of 20 minutes four times a week during exercise.

It is important to note that achieving the minimum training effect—20 minutes at or above your THR four times a week—is just that, the minimum. The longer and harder you train, within reason, the better shape you'll be in. Just remember to start slowly and work your way up. In physical fitness, as in all good things in life, there are no shortcuts. Only a sustained effort over time will produce the results you seek.

3) Choose an Aerobic Exercise: Aerobic exercises must get your heart pumping at your THR and also be an activity, or combination of activities, that interests you enough so you'll stick with it over time. Jogging, swimming, bicycling, walking, jumping rope, and roller-skating are good examples. The step aerobics classes so popular at local health clubs are an excellent way to both improve your overall aerobic capacity and tone up your muscles.

4) Add Strength and Flexibility Training: Aerobic exercise isn't enough. You need to train your muscles and increase flexibility, too. This means weight training or calisthenics such as push-ups, pull-ups, sit-ups, and stretching. When using weights, concentrate on the main muscle groups—legs, back, shoulders, arms, chest, and stomach. However, don't lose sight of the fact that the most important muscle in your body is your heart. It is best strengthened through aerobic exercise.

SPECIFICITY TRAINING

As hunting season nears, it's time to add what exercise physiologists call "specificity training"—exercises designed to improve the performance of a specific task—to your general exercise program. Because wilderness elk hunters spend lots of time hiking and climbing while carrying a loaded pack, they should add exercises that simulate these activities to their basic fitness program. For example, I go for long walks in early summer, starting out for an hour or so at a good pace while wearing a 20-pound daypack. As the season gets closer, I start carrying my backpack with increasingly heavy loads, working up to 100 pounds, which is about what my hunting gear and a packload of boned-out elk meat will weigh. I don't carry that every day, but I try to get my muscles used to that load. It's also important to train not only on flat ground, but on inclines as well. Elk hunting is primarily up-and-down work, in which you'll be climbing and hiking most of the time, so be sure to include exercises that work your climbing muscles when planning your training program. If you jog, be sure to jog up and down some hills. A great running and/or walking exercise is to go up and down the football stadium steps at your local high school or college. If you lift weights, squats, toe raises, and lunges will strengthen the climbing muscles in your legs.

IT WON'T HAPPEN OVERNIGHT

One secret of getting into shape is to realize that it isn't going to happen overnight. Don't overdo it early on. Plan on making the exercise program a part of your daily routine. Start out too fast and you might injure yourself. Make exercise an unpleasant chore and you won't stick with it. When things get grim and I don't feel like doing my exercise for the day, I think of the mountains, the elk, and the challenge of the coming season. That's often enough motivation to get me up and at 'em.

But more important, as a fit individual you'll be able to enjoy your elk hunt to the fullest. With your mind totally focused on the task at hand, when your guide or hunting partner says that the trophy of your dreams is just over the next ridge, you'll simply say, "We're not there yet?" and not, "I don't think I can make it."

MENTAL TOUGHNESS

The odds are against you when you go elk hunting. In most states, success rates on general bulls-only hunts are below 25 percent. Even in some of the better areas of the West, and even if you have a special tag or license for a limited-entry unit or special late-season hunt, bagging a bull is never a sure thing.

What that means is that on a typical elk hunt, you're going to be spending more time looking *for* elk than you are looking *at* elk. There may be days when you don't see any elk at all, let alone a legal bull.

Anyone can keep his head in the game when there are lots of elk to look at. When someone gets lucky and shoots an elk the first or second day, it's easy to be upbeat and excited. But when the hunting gets tough, when the elk seem to vanish into the bowels of the mountain, when the weather turns nasty, it's a lot tougher to keep the excitement going. That's where mental preparation comes in.

A positive attitude is always important in big game hunting, but especially so with elk. Hunters who have a positive outlook on their experience are always more willing to climb another mountain, go look around one more corner, dive into one more stand of

When the food runs low, and you have to prospect for water from underground seeps, will your mental attitude remain positive? Such is the nature of wilderness elk hunting.

dark timber, than those who are dejected and ready to give up. Those with positive attitudes are also much more fun to have in camp, adding to the total hunting experience. One bad attitude can bring down an entire camp, and when that happens, everyone has a more difficult time hunting at peak efficiency.

An elk hunt I took into the Purcell Mountains of British Columbia a few years ago is a good example. We were hunting prime country during the peak of the rut. We just knew we were going to get into some good bulls, and had 10 full days to get the job done. I bugled in a small 4×5 bull on the first evening, but we decided to pass on him. We all had stars in our eyes, and visions of big bulls dancing in our heads. But for the next week, the weather went bad, and the hunting got as tough as it can get. The bulls stayed in the dark timber, the snows came, then the rains and the fog, and we had a helluva time just finding elk. But during this whole time, no

Elk hunting can be tough work, with lots of rough country to cover. Author shot this nice bull only after dogging it for miles in steep country with thin air.

Packing elk meat out of the wilderness is hard work. You not only have to be in shape to find elk, but to get several hundred pounds of meat back to the trailhead.

Wilderness elk hunting is one of the most exciting and rewarding, yet challenging, adventures the West has to offer. But when you walk up to your first downed bull elk, your first thought will be, "Holy smokes! Now what?" Are you up to the task?

one let his chin drop or contaminated camp with a bad attitude. Each day we rode forth, expecting that this was the day we'd put it all together and finally tag a bull.

We never did get a shot at a bull on that trip. What we did do was decide to change our luck, move camp, and hunt some high-country mule deer. The result was a pair of the biggest mule deer bucks I've ever seen taken, both shot on the last day of the trip. The key to our success was our attitude. We enjoyed each other's company, marveled at some spectacular scenery, and hunted hard every day, knowing that success was always right around the next corner.

It can be the same for you. Before you go elk hunting, you must realize that if your hunt goes about the same as most average elk hunts, it's going to be a long week. It will be hard work, with lots of tough country to cover. In all likelihood the weather will turn lousy for at least part of the time. You'll probably be wet, cold, and miserable at least once or twice. More than once you'll dream of a hot shower, clean socks, and a pizza with everything on top.

But that's all part of the trip, the thing that makes elk hunting the wonderful, magical experience it is. By being mentally prepared for the worst, you'll hunt at your best. You'll enjoy your time in the woods, and you'll be a positive factor in the enjoyment of your buddies, too. No matter what happens, you'll drag yourself out of your sleeping bag every morning, ready to go get 'em. When it's all said and done, you'll have wonderful stories to tell for years to come, not negative memories that reflect dark moods.

Staying sharp mentally: It's not always easy, but it's so important. Leave your troubles and worries in town. They'll be there waiting for you when you get home.

4

ELK HUNTING ON YOUR OWN

S ince I shot my first bull elk in 1981 in Idaho's Selway-Bitterroot Wilderness Area, I have seen the face of elk hunting, and the nature of the elk themselves, evolve. The elk of today are not the same as the elk of 30 years ago. They've been educated by constant exposure to hunters, and are harder to find and to hunt today than ever before. Still, thanks to modern game management and increasing numbers of elk, it is possible for anyone to successfully hunt them — if they first understand what such a hunt entails, and how to properly plan and execute such a trip.

The keys to my own elk hunting successes can be boiled down to three words: *planning* and *hard work*. Planning is not the most exciting part of a hunting trip; finding elk, and getting into a position for a shot, are. But without careful planning, once you get into the mountains you'll just be spinning your wheels. Any success you may have will be the result of nothing more than luck. And are you willing to let that be the determining factor in your hunt? I'm not. While luck is a big part of any hunting trip, I like to make my own as much as possible. I do this by planning. Then, once I have a game plan, I'm willing to physically work hard at making it a success.

Why is planning so important? Because elk hunting is a variation of the old needle-in-a-haystack game. You have to find one before you can shoot it, and finding elk is by far the hardest part of the whole undertaking. Elk are herd animals, and while the entire mountain may be good elk country, the herd will only be in a small pocket at any given time. Once you've found the elk, hunting them is really not tremendously difficult, if you don't screw it up. It's the finding that can get tricky.

Maps are the bible of the do-it-yourself elk hunter. Both larger-scale U.S. Forest Service and BLM maps, as well as smaller-scale topographic maps, are invaluable.

Careful planning is important even if you live close to good elk country. But if, like most nonresident elk hunters, you live hundreds or thousands of miles away from your hunting area, planning is critical. Your hunting time is limited, and you won't be able to physically scout the area prior to the season. You can't afford to waste a single day of your hunt wandering around aimlessly. You need a game plan that you have confidence in.

While I don't want to downplay the quality of a good guided hunt, I like hunting on my own for several reasons. First, I can hunt the way I want to hunt, a way that suits my personality and style. On an outfitted hunt, you have to hunt the guide's way. Also, on a do-it-yourself hunt, you can spend as much time as you want bagging your elk. Guided hunts have a restricted time frame, and may not be long enough to get the job done given the often fickle nature of elk. More important, when I hunt on my own, I can hunt anywhere I want. If the elk aren't in one area, I can pack up and move. On guided hunts, you're often stuck hunting only one relatively small area, where the guide has permission.

ELK ARE NOT DEER

Before you begin the planning process, understand that elk are not deer, and therefore must be hunted completely differently. A common mistake many first-time elk hunters make is to hunt for elk the same way they hunt mule deer. You may use some of the same basic hunting techniques—glassing, for example—but in a different fashion.

Mule deer are browsers. They are also homebodies, preferring to spend their lives in a relatively small area, moving only when the snow gets deep, the food or water runs out, or they are pushed out. Elk, on the other hand, are grazers. They are constantly on the move, looking for enough high-quality food to satisfy their large appetites. A good mule deer buck may spend most of his life in an area

37

When planning a hunt, remember that elk are not mule deer, and must be hunted differently. You need to cover much more country to locate elk herds.

smaller than one or two square miles. Elk may move five miles a day just feeding. They can also move three times that distance under certain conditions.

For that reason, you have to hunt each species differently. If you are mule deer hunting and locate a buck or group of bucks, for example, you can hunt the same general area day after day and be fairly confident that you can find them again and again. But with elk, they are here today, gone tomorrow. They may be in the same drainage, but one day at the head, the next day five miles down the canyon, the next day five miles from there.

When I'm deer hunting, I put much more emphasis on fresh sign than I do when elk hunting. If I find a fresh elk rub, or fresh elk tracks in the afternoon that I think were made that morning, that only tells me where the elk *were*. I want to know where they *are*. Fresh sign only confirms what my prehunt research told me: that there are elk in my drainage. But until I find a track with an elk standing right in the middle of it, I still have to move. If I were deer hunting and found the same sign, I'd hunt the area in which the sign was located, confident the animals were still close by. The exception is if I find wet, steaming droppings, or a wet spot made by an elk urinating. Then I know the elk are very close, and it's time to slow down and hunt cautiously.

STEP ONE: GAME DEPARTMENTS

It's important to realize that many states offer "special-draw" or "limited entry" elk hunts, in which hunter numbers are restricted, and therefore the chances for success are greater than they are during general hunting seasons. Not a season goes by that I don't apply for a special elk tag in several states, hoping to draw one. In some years I get lucky, in most I don't. But if you don't apply, you can't draw a tag, and if you don't draw, the state refunds your money minus a small application fee. It's a no-lose situation.

At the same time, I begin researching areas that I'm thinking about hunting. Books, magazine articles, maps, harvest statistics, state game regulations, and people are the building blocks of any solid research program. My goal is to paint a picture of the hunting area, so that I know what to expect when I get there. I don't want to waste precious days learning the country that can be better spent searching for elk.

Step one is to write, call, or check the Web sites of the game departments in the states you are considering hunting and ask for the coming year's regulations. Seasons vary greatly by state, even in different units in each state, and you need this information. Also, ask for recent harvest statistics and tag drawing odds. This is all public information, and should be available to you. These numbers are just the beginning, but they help paint a broad portrait of hunter distribution, harvest by area, and tag drawing odds, which together give you a foundation upon which to build your plan.

I find that magazine articles, books on elk hunting, and even newspaper articles can sometimes offer clues to the hunting potential of a certain area. When I find helpful articles, I file them away for reference.

One of the biggest boons in recent years to researching a hunt in a new area is the Internet. All state and Canadian province game departments that offer elk hunting have Internet Web sites. Here you can find lots of information quickly, and it's generally very fresh, up-to-the-minute stuff that is valuable in planning your hunt. Regulations, tag application dates, special-draw hunts, fees, and so on are all here. In many cases, so are harvest statistics and even hunter success rates by individual hunt unit. Hunting Web sites can also produce useful information, without building up a massive long-distance telephone bill. A listing of various state agencies can be found in this book's appendix section.

STEP TWO: MAPS, MAPS, MAPS

Once you've narrowed your choice down to a general area in a specific state, it's time for maps. The U.S. Forest Service and Bureau of Land Management both have maps of publicly owned lands within specific states that can help you locate roads, major trails and trailheads, national park and private land boundaries, campgrounds, and so on. I like general state maps, too, ones that show an entire state. By using these maps I can begin to get a picture of the areas I'm thinking about hunting.

Later in the process it will be time for the smaller-scale topographic maps available from the U.S. Geological Survey. These finely detailed maps show too small an area to be of any use in the initial planning process, so hold off on buying them until you've

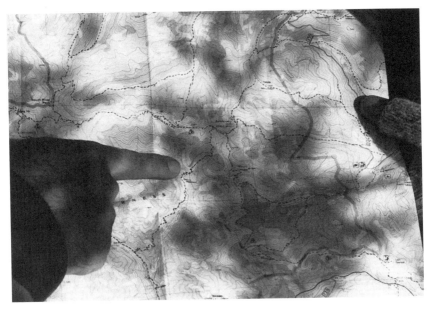

Using topo maps, you can find areas that just seem to have elk saying, "Here we are!" Look for edge cover in fairly tough country, and open basins on high-altitude north slopes. Also check for roads, trails, and trailheads.

narrowed down your options a bit. I use the larger maps to help me narrow down my potential hunting area, then topo maps to zero in on places I think elk will actually be in that area.

I can't emphasize enough the importance of maps, both in the planning process and the actual hunt itself. They are my eyes, helping me find elk before I have actually seen the area. Without them, I feel blind. Map sources can be found in this book's appendix section.

STEP THREE: PEOPLE

The final stage of the planning process is talking with people. Maps give you a general overview of an area, but people can fill in the blanks and give you an accurate, up-to-date picture of what the area is really like.

The critical step in planning is telephone research. When calling government officials, try and speak with local, not regional, sources that can give you specific, up-to-date information on the elk hunting in that area.

"Up-to-date" is the key phrase here. Maps are invaluable, but you'll rarely, if ever, find a map that is up-to-date. New roads, trails, logging operations, and so on may not be shown on your maps, but people familiar with the area can fill you in on these, and other, conditions that will affect elk movements.

Who should you talk with? State game department biologists are great. When I call game departments, I try to work my way down the organizational ladder, not up it. I don't want the man in charge of half the state—I want the local biologist who oversees a specific forest or drainage that I'm thinking about hunting. The same holds true for game wardens, forest service personnel, and so on. These people work right in the area and can fill me in on current conditions. They may be hard to locate, and it may cost a few dollars in long-distance phone calls, but it's money and time well spent.

I also try to talk with other hunters, local taxidermists, and any other contacts I can think of. I ask as many different people as I can the same questions, then "balance" their answers in my mind. The bottom line is a picture of the country I want to hunt.

STEP FOUR: HUNTING THE AREA

Your research should give you a good picture of the area in which you've decided to hunt, including information about the elk herd, terrain, access, probable hunter pressure, and so on. And you can place your hunt from this data. For example, say the area you've decided to hunt has lots of high alpine meadows loaded with lush grass. There are few trails, but good road access at lower elevations, and hunter numbers over opening weekend are generally high. In this situation, a good opening-day strategy might be to hike in to a saddle near the alpine meadow before first light. You'll be searching for elk that may be feeding there at daybreak, but also be in a position to intercept any elk pushed by hunters moving in from the road.

You get the picture—or at least you should, if your planning has been thorough. Planning not only tells me where the best elk hunting should be, but where the elk should be living in a specific drainage, and how to hunt that drainage. It's not foolproof—what in elk hunting is?—but it beats stumbling around the mountains without a clue.

HOW TO HUNT ON YOUR OWN

After planning, the other key to hunting elk on your own is mobility. You must be mobile to hunt elk successfully. Elk are not deer; they cover lots of ground in a day, and so must you. On the average, I figure I hike between 8 and 12 miles each day in search of elk, and sometimes more. It's hard work, but necessary.

When I plan my elk hunts, I try to avoid trailheads leading from major parking areas. These are easy access routes, used by a lot of elk hunters. I also avoid carrying a heavy backpack filled with a week's worth of supplies. Instead, I carry only two or three days' worth of the barest essentials at a time.

Why? Because mobility is the key, I travel light. While I sometimes set up a backcountry base camp and hunt from there, I often do not. Instead I use my truck as base camp, which gives me tremendous flexibility in hunting lots of country. Here's how I do it.

Using my maps, I pick good-looking areas between major trailheads to hunt. I then park my truck away from the trailhead, load my backpack with three days' worth of supplies, and take off cross-country. I hunt out of a bivouac camp, carrying camp with me all day long. I make a big loop through the country, and in three days can hunt up to 30 miles or more. If I find the elk, I hunt them. If I really get into them, I may come out, resupply, then go back and plan to stay for a while. If I don't find elk, I come back to the truck, drive on to another area I've already researched, and start again. By

Mobility is the key to locating herds of elk. One good way to cover the maximum amount of ground and not waste any time in an elkless area is to bivouac out from your truck, carrying a small pack with a maximum of three days' supplies.

doing this I'm not spending time hunting country in which there are no elk.

The areas I like to hunt are usually in wilderness or semiwilderness areas which, because of the nature of the country, few people will be hunting. On my topographic maps, I look for fairly rough country that has lots of "edge" cover—trees that meet meadows, well-defined benches along steep hillsides, and so on. I hunt structure the way a bass fisherman works a lake. The bass fisherman knows that fish will travel along certain edge cover routes, and he fishes them. I hunt the same irregularities in terrain, looking for elk. I look for high, open basins on west- and north-facing slopes. Bedding areas are usually in lodgepole pine thickets, in cool, dark areas. During the rut, I look for level benches with firm, dry footing. I believe elk have traditional rutting areas and will use them year after year.

This stick-and-move style of hunting isn't for everyone. But for those who can physically do it, it can be highly effective.

Another tactic I like to use is what I call "run and gun" hunting. I am a very aggressive elk hunter. I believe in pushing the animals hard once I've found them. I like to get right in among them, whether I'm hunting with a bow or a rifle. I want the elk to be reacting to me, not the other way around.

Sometimes I'll come across a herd with a good bull in it, but the animals will begin moving away from me. When that happens, I try to loop around them, often running a mile or more to get ahead of the herd. I know that they will probably stay at the same elevation as they travel around the mountain, so I set up ahead at that elevation and wait, searching for them with both my eyes and ears. If I can find the herd again—and I usually can—and can sit still and let the elk filter all around me, I can usually get a shot at the bull I want. This works when both rifle and archery hunting.

EQUIPMENT SELECTION

Equipment selection is critical for stick-and-move hunting. I don't want to carry one extra ounce of weight that I don't have to.

I really like lightweight, streamlined, internal-frame backpacks, leaving the larger, external frame pack in the truck until I kill an elk and have to haul out meat. I rarely take a stove, choosing instead to use foods that require no cooking on my three-day swings. My sleeping bag weighs only two pounds. A top-quality ground pad, like those from ThermaRest, is a must. In early bow seasons, a one-man bivvy shelter protects me from wind and water. During later rifle seasons, when it gets cold and wet, a small, lightweight two-man tent replaces the bivvy.

In my backpack go my maps, a quart of water, knife and steel, minimal first-aid kit, small tube of petroleum jelly, fire-starter materials, small roll of electrician's tape, roll of fluorescent flagging material, and a lightweight headlamp. I always carry four cheesecloth elk quarter bags for meat care.

The total weight of my pack is about 20 pounds. In addition to that, I carry my weapon and binoculars, usually full-sized 10×40 glasses. My boots are lightweight, and I don't carry spare socks, underwear, or even a toothbrush. Unless you've hiked steep, high-altitude elk country, you can't fully appreciate how much difference a few ounces make. Take what you need, but nothing more.

Bob Robb has taken over a dozen bulls on do-it-yourself hunts. Planning, persistence, and a cover-lots-of-ground, never-say-die philosophy are the keys to his success.

Elk hunting on your own is a real adventure. It's also hard work. But the smell of success is never sweeter than when you plan your own hunt, execute that plan, and everything falls into place. When that happens, you'll have earned one of North America's most prized hunting trophies, fair and square.

It just doesn't get any better.

5

HOW TO BOOK A GUIDED HUNT (*with Al Kuntz*)

Booking a guided hunting trip can be as much of an adventure as the actual hunt itself. There are lots of guides out there, some good and some not so good, all competing for your money. Al Kuntz can help you get through the maze. In addition to being a booking agent with a long track record of arranging successful and enjoyable hunts around the world for his many clients, Kuntz is a serious hunter himself, having taken more than 30 Pope & Young record-book animals. He only books hunts he has personally taken, so he knows all his outfitters like family. He's been around the block, knows what it takes to make individual clients happy, and his advice is worth heeding. For more information on his services, contact him at Al's Worldwide Adventures, P.O. Box 38, Scandia, MN 55073; toll-free 1-888/331-5014; or visit his Web site, www.alsadventures.com.

"**W**hile many sportsmen hunt elk on their own each fall, thousands enlist the services of a professional guide or outfitter to help them make their dream come true," says Al Kuntz. "With thousands of guides and outfitters competing for your elk hunting business, there's a lot to sort through. When booking a guided hunt, the one thing you do *not* want to do is give someone your money, and your dreams, without carefully researching your options—and their business—first."

Al Kuntz of Al's Worldwide Adventures not only books lots of outfitted elk hunts, he's a serious elk hunter himself. Kuntz took this superb 6 × 7 bull with his bow on an outfitted horseback hunt into an Idaho wilderness area.

YOU GET WHAT YOU PAY FOR

Kuntz emphasizes that when it comes to guided hunting in general, and elk hunting in particular, you definitely get what you pay for.

"Here's what I mean," he says. "Most people looking to book their first guided elk hunt are trying to save some money. That's understandable. And so they look at wilderness elk hunts that cost someplace between $2000 and $4000, plus a nonresident hunting license, elk tag, transportation, and the value of their vacation time from work. But when you get down to it, the success rates on most of these types of fair-chase wilderness elk hunts are low, usually less than 33 percent.

"So let's say you are the 'average' guy," Kuntz continues. "That means it would take three of these hunts before you got your first elk. The chances are good this bull would be a small raghorn bull, not the trophy-class mature bull you've been dreaming of. You've got three years and somewhere between $10,000 and $15,000 invested in this elk, which may or may not be the bull of your dreams."

A better scenario, Kuntz said, is for the average hunter to wait a year or two, save his money, and go on a top-quality—and more expensive—guided hunt on private land or a remote wilderness area, where the chances of a crack at a mature bull are much higher.

"These hunts can cost between $5000 and $10,000, plus the licenses and so on. However, the success rates are much higher, generally 90 percent on the hunts I book; plus the accommodations, food, and so on are of a higher standard. And this is for shots at 6×6 or better bulls. Now the hunter has the same amount of money—or less—invested in his elk hunt, but he has wasted no time, gone first cabin, and had the chance to learn about elk and elk hunting by being able to see and be around elk almost every day he is in the field. This is knowledge he can take with him on future hunts, even

Wilderness elk outfitters are busy people. Long before the season opens they are working hard, setting up camps, repairing equipment, and scouting for game.

Before speaking with outfitters, ask yourself, "Why do I want to go on this trip?" The answer will help determine the kind of outfitter you select. Jim Nelson wanted a trophy-class bull with his bow, and booked a private ranch hunt in a Montana archery-only area. The result? A 6 × 6 that scored 378 Pope & Young points.

those he does on his own. They may cost more up front, but in the long run the investment is worth it."

WHAT ABOUT DROP CAMPS?

One popular method of "guided" elk hunting is the drop camp. In a drop camp situation, an outfitter will provide the hunters with almost all the equipment—camp, cooking gear, and so on—and set the camp up in an area he recommends as holding fair numbers of elk. The hunters are then left to their own devices. Costs are usually a third to a half of what a guided hunt would cost.

Drop camps are a good option for experienced elk hunters, Kuntz says, but should be avoided by the first-timer.

"Drop camps can work well for those who know how to hunt elk, but for those who have not tried it yet they can be a bad deal. For one thing, a big key to successful mountain hunting is knowing the country and the habits of the animals that live there. Drop camp hunters may get some 'get started' advice from the outfitter, but once the game begins, things change, and unless you know the area you won't know how to adapt quickly to those changes. You don't know where the wallows, water sources, and trails are, how the thermal currents flow and winds blow, and so on. By the time the average novice has found the elk—not the bulls, just the elk—his week's hunt is over.

"There are other problems," Kuntz continues. "Elk hunting is hard work, and when you have to cook for yourself, bring your own food, and so on, you end up taking a lot of hunting time to handle basic camp chores. If you shoot an elk you have the meat care chores to tend to. And believe me, if you have never had to butcher and pack an elk off a steep high-altitude mountain, you don't know how miserable this can be!

"Save your drop camp hunting for later in your career, when you have some elk hunting under your belt. You'll be glad you did."

Use both state hunting regulations and outfitter brochures as a first step in giving you an idea of a particular hunting area, as well as the outfitter's services and prices.

ASSESS YOUR PHYSICAL LIMITATIONS

The keys to finding the right outfitter for your guided hunt include deciding what your goals are, being realistic about your physical limitations, and being honest with yourself about the kind of elk that will make you happy.

"Of course your budget is a key factor, but again, you get what you pay for in guided elk hunting," Kuntz says. "Decide what your goals are, then save until you can meet them. But above and beyond that, I encourage all prospective elk hunters to realistically assess their physical abilities before going any further. Believe me, wilderness elk hunting can be the toughest thing you have ever done. Most failures on mountain hunts occur because the client simply could not handle it physically. Let's face it, we all promise ourselves we are going to lose a little weight and tone up, but the reality is that most of us will not do either to a large degree just for a hunting trip.

"After years of hearing about these problems from both guides and clients, my solution as a booking agent was to begin finding quality hunts at lower elevations with less physical demands on the client," Kuntz says. "I found that my clients all wanted a crack at a good bull without the need for an oxygen mask and a paramedic team! I encourage my clients to consider the physical abilities of the *least* fit member of their group when booking a hunt. Take into consideration everyone's age, weight, health, fitness level, and mountain hunting experience before deciding where and how to hunt.

"With this information in hand, as a booking agent I can then present the group with multiple options of quality hunts that balance their desire for a chance at a good bull with their budget and physical abilities. There are all sorts of elk hunts out there. You can hunt from sea level to 10,000 feet; use trucks, ATVs, horses, llamas, or backpacks and your own feet as modes of transportation; hunt public or private land; go after a cow elk, any bull, or trophy bulls only. You can camp in a small tent, snug mountain cabin, or fancy lodge. Your hunt can last anywhere from 5 to 14 days, have one guide per hunter or one guide for every two hunters, and spend between $3500 and $12,000 per hunter."

INCREASING YOUR ODDS

It is easy to see how the whole process can be confusing. As Kuntz says, hunting is a game of playing the odds. While things don't come together every day, with careful planning and research you can tip the odds in your favor.

"Clients should understand that no matter how much they want an elk, or how much money they have paid for their hunt, there are no guarantees of success in fair-chase hunting," Kuntz says. "You may be hunting with an outfitter who produces a 50 percent success rate, but this year you may be one of the 50 percent who doesn't get his elk.

"That said, generally speaking the more you pay for your elk hunt, the better your chances for success. The reasons for that are simple. On the more expensive hunts you'll usually find yourself hunting some sort of exclusive hunting area, which can be either private land or a remote wilderness area in which the outfitter holds exclusive guiding rights and the area sees little, if any, resident hunting pressure. The area will have a high elk population, with a good bull/cow ratio and a good number of mature bulls. Tags will be guaranteed, meaning you do not have to try to draw one of the limited-entry tags in the better public land areas that have become so difficult to draw. There will be experienced guides who know the area, quality food and accommodations, and well-maintained equipment. The terrain will be relatively gentle, you have some sort of flexibility

Top-notch outfitters have back-up plans in case hunting slows in your area. They can pack up and move you to a different region quickly and efficiently.

in your hunt dates, and there will be several different ways to efficiently hunt the elk."

TROPHY ELK HUNTING

One reason many elk hunters employ a guide is that they believe their chances of taking a trophy 6 × 6 bull will be better on that hunt than if they hunted on their own. This may or may not be true, according to Kuntz.

"All serious hunters would love to have a big bull hanging in their home," he says. "If that is your goal, then you have to be realistic about it and consider all the factors involved in such a quest.

"First, a mature bull elk is a master of survival. He didn't reach 7 to 10 years of age by being dumb. He knows his home territory like you know the back of your hand. Generally speaking he lives in remote, rugged, nasty country—far from the beaten path—that is extremely difficult for a human to navigate. In this type of terrain a quality outfitter can make the difference between having a good chance at finding your dream bull and no chance at all."

Kuntz also notes that not every state or Canadian province grows large antlers on a good percentage of their mature elk. If you want to hunt the biggest bulls, you need to book a hunt in the states where they live. While a giant bull can come from any western state, the best chance at finding one is in states like Arizona, New Mexico, Nevada, and Montana and Wyoming in units near Yellowstone Park. "These states grow huge bulls," Kuntz says. "They aren't found in every drainage, but the average size of a big bull is larger than the average size found in other states."

The problem with hunting in many of the top trophy-producing areas of these, as well as other, western states is the fact that elk licenses are sold on quota, meaning that you have to draw a tag before you can hunt. And the odds of drawing one of these coveted tags is extremely low. In many states, including New Mexico, Montana, Colorado, and Idaho, as well as in British Columbia and Alberta, hiring an outfitter can eliminate this problem because many outfitters are allocated a given number of tags each year. You are guaranteed a tag when you book a hunt with them.

"The western tag-drawing game is complicated as heck," Kuntz says. "Every state has different rules, regulations, fees, deadlines for applications, and so on. It is easy to get confused. Booking with a guide who hunts either public land or, in many cases, private ranch land guarantees you'll get your tag *and* be hunting in an area where elk numbers are high, bull/cow ratios are good, success rates are very high, and the chances at a nice 6×6 or better bull are as good as they get in fair-chase hunting."

YOUR BEST CHANCE AT A BIG BULL

Back in the 1970s, hunters were allowed to hunt the rut, or "bugle season" as many call it, with rifles. Then more and more elk hunters began learning how to call bulls; when combined with a centerfire rifle that can cleanly kill the biggest bull a quarter mile away, the result was that the number of mature bulls killed by sportsmen skyrocketed. Eventually, state fish and game departments had to curtail general rifle seasons on public lands during the September rut. These hunts are reserved for bowhunters today.

Despite this, you can still hunt bugling bulls with a centerfire rifle or modern in-line muzzleloader that can kill a bull elk at 200 steps with relative ease. Some private land hunts are held in this fashion, as are many of the state's various muzzleloader-only seasons. The very best hunt of this type, according to Kuntz, is in the wilderness of British Columbia.

"For the person looking for a trophy bull elk, it does not get any better than this," Kuntz says. "Hunters stay in comfortable cabins, eat like kings, hunt with horses or on foot at an elevation of between 2000 and 4000 feet, and are squired around by excellent guides.

Tags are guaranteed. The area only permits the harvest of 6×6 bulls or better, and the average bull of this type taken scores between 280 and 340 Boone and Crockett points. The area is so remote it gets virtually no other hunting pressure. Success rates are 90 percent-plus. The hunt can also be combined with moose, mountain goat, black bear, or grizzly bear if a guy wants to spend some more money and stay longer. The hunts last between 5 and 14 days, the season runs August 15 to October 15, and both firearms and archery equipment are allowed.

"This is my favorite trophy elk hunt of all," Kuntz continues. "But there are similar hunts in other places. Many of the private ranch hunts in New Mexico, where landowner tags guarantee the client a license, produce whopper bulls where the hunting is done from a truck, and clients stay in fancy lodges.

Quality guided elk hunts matched to each hunter's needs and budget are an excellent way to find success. But, as Al Kuntz says, you definitely get what you pay for in guided elk hunting. The biggest bulls and highest success rates generally come from private land or limited-entry areas.

"Granted, these hunts do not give you the same wilderness-type experience as a horseback hunt into the Rocky Mountains. But they do give you the best chance at a big bull with the least amount of physical discomfort. It all boils down to the client deciding what his priorities are, then finding the right hunt that will give him the best chance at meeting those goals."

10 QUESTIONS

Here are 10 questions you should ask any prospective elk outfitter or booking agent before making a final decision.

1) *What are the species with top trophy potential in your area?* If you want a big elk, with an average mule deer as your secondary goal, but the area has only mediocre elk and a few big mulies, you're probably hunting in the wrong place.

2) *How many actual hunting days are there?* On a 10-day hunt, you may have one day's travel time each way in and out of the hunting area, cutting the actual hunt time to eight days. If you're stranded in base camp for extra days because the outfitter is having problems, will he allow you to extend your hunt to compensate for missed days afield that were not your fault? The outfitter can't control the weather, but he should be in control of his equipment, staff, and scheduling.

3) *How many hunters and support people will there be in camp?* To avoid overcrowding, you want to know how many other hunters will be in hunting camp. Also ask if your guide doubles as the cook, horse wrangler, and woodcutter. Generally, but not always, it's better if the guide does nothing except take you hunting.

4) *How many hunters per guide?* Do you have your guide all to yourself, or will you be sharing him with another client? Though it costs more, it's almost always more productive to

hunt one-on-one. If you get to camp and your one-on-one hunt is suddenly a two-on-one affair, resolve the problem with the outfitter immediately.

5) *How long have you been hunting in your area?* I prefer to hunt with people who have been outfitting an area for at least three seasons, and therefore know the lay of the land and area game movements well. Also, the outfitter will rarely be taking you hunting himself. You want a guide with experience hunting both the area and the species you're targeting. Don't settle for a first-year guide as your primary guide.

6) *Bowhunters: Are your guides experienced bowhunters themselves? Have they successfully guided bowhunters before?* It's important for bowhunters to have a guide who understands the unique requirements of hunting with archery tackle.

7) *What percentage of your clients are repeat customers?* If the outfitter is lousy and there is little game in his area, he probably has few repeat clients. Repeat business is one indicator of a reputable outfit.

8) *What does the hunt package cost?* You'll be quoted a hunt cost of, say, $4000 for a horseback wilderness elk hunt. Now ask about any hidden costs, such as licenses and tags (rarely included in the hunt price), trophy and meat care, tips and gratuities, additional charges if you take another animal, and so on. Is there a trophy fee for actually taking an animal, or for taking an animal that scores exceptionally well by record book standards?

9) *Do you have references I can contact?* Ask for a list not only of successful clients but also of clients who did not get game on their hunt. Ask for references within the past three years. Spend a few bucks and call several, and ask lots of questions regarding all aspects of the hunt. If an outfitter won't provide references, avoid him like the plague.

10) *Do you have a written hunt contract?* Years ago, a handshake and deposit were enough. Today, they're not. Make sure the outfitter has a prepared hunt agreement that spells out everything in writing, including hunt cost, duration, species to be hunted, guide-to-hunter ratio, specific hunt dates, his cancellation policy, and so on. Make sure he has liability insurance. Check with the state to make sure he is licensed and bonded. Before signing the contract, have *all* your questions answered. Outfitters who don't have the time to spend with you on these matters are more interested in your money than your satisfaction. Hunt with someone else.

6

CALLING ALL ELK
(with *Chad Schearer*)

Just 30 years old, Chad Schearer has been fascinated by, and seriously hunting for, elk since he was 12 near his central Montana home. He started calling elk at a young age, and won the Rocky Mountain Elk Foundation eastern United States championships in 1996 and 1997, as well as the prestigious RMEF World Elk Calling championships in 1997. He's on the staffs of Knight & Hale Game Calls, Golden Eagle Archery, Satellite Broadheads, Knight Muzzleloader, Code Blue Scents, and Easton Technical Products. Chad and wife Marsha own and operate Central Montana Outfitters, a first-class outfit specializing in elk, mule deer, antelope, and varmint hunting, as well as fly fishing for trout. You can reach him at Box 6655, Great Falls, MT 59406; 406/799-7984; Web address www.cmontanaoutfitters.com.)

Chad Schearer is a former world elk calling champion and successful Montana elk outfitter who has called in hundreds of elk since he was 12 years old.

"**O**ne of the things I've learned over the years is that competition calling is a different world than calling when you're actually hunting elk," Schearer says. "Really, it is harder to convince judges you're the best than it is calling a bull elk in. In the RMEF competitions, you have one minute for cow sounds, one minute for bull sounds, and two minutes for making any elk sounds you can. The big difference is that when we're competing, we're trying to sound like a large, aggressive herd bull; but when you are hunting, you have to tone your calling down to a more submissive level. The raspy, growly calling that wins contests can be counterproductive when hunting, actually scaring most bulls away. Competition is fun, and you'll learn a lot, but how we hunt and how we compete are two different worlds. You have to be a woodsman to consistently kill elk."

Schearer notes that in addition to mastering a few basic elk sounds, you need to "hang loose" when hunting to be successful. "The biggest thing I have learned after calling in hundreds of bulls is that you must be flexible. You have to be willing and able to make instant adjustments when you're working a bull. No two situations are ever exactly the same. I ask lots of people for their ideas on what works for them; it's amazing what you can learn from other hunters, even those with little experience. Another thing that has helped me become a better elk hunter is spring turkey hunting. This is almost identical to elk hunting, except that you don't have to watch the wind. You do have to be more careful with movement, which has helped me fine-tune my setups for elk. You learn not be sloppy. I recommend that all hunters planning a fall elk hunt with calling involved do some spring turkey hunting."

Chad also emphasizes the need for preseason calling practice. "People need to practice their calling before the season. They'll shoot their bows or firearms for months and work hard to get into good physical condition, but they won't blow their calls until two weeks before the hunt. I have had a lot of people tell me, 'Well, by the end of the season my calling started to sound good.' It's too late! You need to be in midseason calling form from the get-go. Buy all your new calls in winter or early spring and start practicing right away. Rent or buy a video of live elk calling and watch what the animals do, and bugle or cow-call back to the TV screen. Try to replicate what the bull is doing. This will help you become a better elk caller. Audiocassette tapes are also super. I listen to them when I'm driving, and practice calling back to the tape. If you can talk on the phone and drive, why can't you use an elk call, too? If you commute by car, why not use your commuting time to practice for a few months before the season opens?"

LOCATING A BULL

"When you start the day off, listen, don't call," Schearer says. "If you hear a bull bugle, you have half the battle won before you've made your first sound. Move in close before you start working him. If you don't hear a bull sound off, your job is to *make* him sound off. To do that, I use a 'locator bugle.' Here I try to sound like a small or young bull. I don't want to get aggressive, and use just three to five high-pitched tones. Don't get real raspy. Just use a simple scale with basic low to high notes. Sometimes I add one or two grunts, but not aggressively. That's because I am trying to challenge a bull without scaring him off. Remember, in some areas a satellite bull can be a nice five- or six-point bull, and if you sound like a giant herd bull you might run off these satellites."

When trying to locate a bull, Chad likes to get up high on a ridge but be near an area where he can set up quickly in case an elk happens to be close. "I like to be able to listen down into multiple

Schearer believes you should never make elk sounds in the woods without being prepared for an elk to come charging in. "You only have to get busted once by being careless to learn this lesson," he said.

canyons," he says. "Never skyline yourself, and always be ready to set up fast. I can't tell you how many times I messed up a hot bull because I had not gotten set up before calling, then had him charge in from a hundred yards away and catch me with my pants down.

"Also, always assume that every bugle you hear is an elk, not another hunter. I have heard some elk sounds that were so awful you would swear they were made by a person trying to bugle for the first time, and they turned out to be from a big bull. The minute you assume it's not a bull, it will be the biggest bull you've ever seen, and he'll walk in on you when you're not ready. I'd rather be called in by someone and look dumb than blow a chance at a bull. Conversely, if you call a person in, be sure to whistle or holler so they know you're a hunter, not a bull. Don't stay hidden.

"Once I have located a bull, the first thing I do is check wind direction," Schearer says. "Wind direction is *always* your primary concern when you're trying to call elk in close. Your setup is just as important as the sounds you are making. Check out *everything* before you try to draw the bull in for a shot. I always carry *Knight & Hale Windfloaters*, a great product that allows me to monitor the wind 30 to 40 yards from me, not just right where I am standing. That way I can set up accordingly."

CHECKING HIS TEMPERATURE

Next, Schearer likes to do what he calls "checking the bull's temperature," determining whether the bull is aggressive or passive in nature. "This determines how I'll work him. If he is passive, I'll be passive, too, and it becomes more of a cat and mouse game that I usually play with a cow call. If he's responding well to a bugle, I'll stick with the bugle, although I may switch over to a cow call and try to coax him in. It's natural for the cow to move toward the bull when they hear the bugle, which is one reason bulls are reluctant to come to a call. The other thing I try to determine is whether or not the

Schearer likes to use his bugle as a locator-type call, trying to check the bull's temperature before deciding how to approach that particular animal.

bull has cows with him. If he hangs up during the calling process, I assume he has cows and probably will not come to me. Then I have to move in as close as I can and begin to try to seduce him with my cow call.

"If the bull is aggressively responding to my calling and sounds like he is getting closer, I'll try to match the tempo of his calling, then slowly increase it," Schearer says. "The goal here is to get him so excited that he becomes overly aggressive and charges right in. When working a bull like this, it is critical to keep monitoring the wind and making sure you are set up to shoot."

Every setup is different, and you have to be able to adjust. "There are little things to remember. For example, I try to set up off a well-defined trail, not in the middle of it, in a spot where I can get the bull to walk uphill to me. Otherwise the chances are good the bull will come right down the trail straight at you, and you won't have a good shot angle. Typically, though, the bull will try to circle you. Why? During the rut, bulls use wallows and urinate all over

Bugling and bull elk go together like bread and butter. While the best bugling occurs during the September rut, Schearer bugles up bulls from August through October.

themselves. I've found that mature herd bulls are more rank smelling than younger bulls. The natural thing for that bull coming to a challenge is to be able to smell the other bull, which will help him know how dominant that bull is, as well as try to smell cows.

"I don't believe the bulls are trying to smell a hunter," Schearer continues. "They're coming to the call because they think you are an elk. But if they get even the smallest whiff of you, they will be gone so fast it will make your head spin. That's why I always carry some Code Blue cow estrus scent in a little spray bottle, which I constantly spritz into the air to mask my scent as well as give the bull a real 'elk' smell."

According to Schearer, the most effective calling tactic is to hunt with a good caller, and to use the buddy system. "Turkey hunters use this all the time, and it works like mad. Set the caller up 50 to 75 yards behind the shooter. That allows the hunter to ambush the bull as he walks in and is focused on where the calling sounds

THE BUDDY SYSTEM. Set the caller up about 50 to 75 yards behind the shooter. As a bull comes in, his attention will be focused on the location of the caller. If he hangs up, as bull elk often do, the shooter should have a perfect opportunity for a 50- to 100-yard shot. The shooter should never call.

are coming from. When a bull comes in he will typically hang up 50 to 75 yards away, which gives the shooter his opportunity. It is also important to remember that the shooter should never call, except maybe to make a cow call to stop the bull for a clear shot." When he's the caller, Chad also likes to move around to give the bull the impression he's a live elk. At times he'll even belly-crawl backwards, trying to make the bull believe a smaller bull has stolen that cow and is leaving with her.

TYPES OF ELK CALLS

There are several different types of elk calls on today's market, all of which will work, depending on the situation. "The more different calls a hunter is competent with, the better his chances," Schearer says. "Sometimes, when one specific call won't get a response, a slightly different tone will. Versatility will pay off in the long run."

The most popular type of call used today is the internal latex diaphragm. These calls are inserted into the mouth and can be used without your hands. This is an especially big advantage for bowhunters, who need both hands free to make a shot when they've called a bull into bow range. There are three basic types of internal diaphragm calls: single, double, and triple reed. Each designation refers to the number of latex reeds in the call.

"Basically, we use a single-reed diaphragm for cow calling because it gives you a single, dulcet tone," Schearer says. "A double-reed call is good for both challenging bulls with medium-level bugling and growling and for making excellent cow sounds. It's the most versatile. A triple-reed call is for making bull sounds only. You can make the triple sound like either a young bull or a herd bull, depending on how much pressure you place on the latex with your tongue and how hard you blow.

"One good feature about some diaphragm calls is that they use different color-coded tapes to help you quickly grab the right call," Schearer notes. "Also, make sure you have a case for your diaphragms; the ones with small holes in the bottom will let your calls dry out and

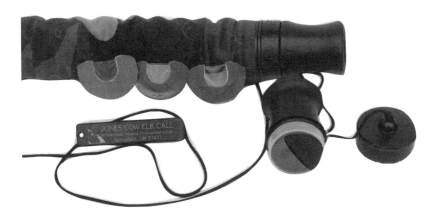

There are several types of elk calls available today. Internal diaphragm calls are the most popular and versatile, while external diaphragm calls are excellent as locator bugles. Rubber band-type cow calls are easy to use, and highly effective, too.

keep them from cracking." Schearer rotates his calls, letting one dry out after a day's use, which helps them last for more than a season. He also recommends storing them in a cool, dark area and not leaving them on the dash of a truck, where the sun can melt them.

Reed-type (external) diaphragm calls are another good choice for both bull and cow sounds. "The downside to these calls is that it is hard to get a really good grunt with them, but they are excellent locator calls," Schearer says. "Don't expect these calls to be very versatile, but carry one of these and a cow call or two, and you have a complete arsenal."

Regardless of whether you use the internal or external diaphragm calls, using low air and tongue pressure on the diaphragm will give you a lower tone. "When the latex starts tickling your tongue, you're at the right spot," Schearer says. "Higher air and tongue pressure give you the higher tones. It's like a musical scale. When I hit the last tone in a bugling sequence I let out all the air, then start grunting, which is a rapid inhaling and exhaling, sort of like hiccups. When using the single diaphragm to make cow sounds, I do an *eeeee-oooo* high-pressure, low-pressure tone. This is very simple to do. Anyone should be able to make basic cow sounds with 10 minutes of practice."

The cow call is the most versatile, and most important, type of call an elk hunter can make, Schearer notes. There are different types of calls that can make excellent cow sounds.

"My favorite for cow sounds is a single-reed internal diaphragm call," Schearer says. "I really like the Knight & Hale single reed because it has a very thick piece of latex, which makes it easy to go soft or loud. The other popular type of cow call is the bite-down call. With this call the hunter simply bites down on the outside of the call's mouthpiece, and controls the tone and pitch with both the pressure of the bite and air pressure. There are several very good bite-down cow calls out there. I like the Knight & Hale Real Cow

Elk make cow sounds all year long, and these calls can work well for you during both gun and bowhunting seasons.

Talker, because it has soft rubber around the mouthpiece that won't hurt your teeth, as well as a great tone. It's easy to blow, and very hunter friendly. When the elk are getting finicky, I'll sometimes mix it up, using both an internal diaphragm and a bite-down call."

The "excited cow" or "hyper hot cow" call is the call of choice in elk hunting today. There are several different makes and models, but they all strive to imitate the "hyper" sound of an estrus cow that wants to be bred right now. "Like deer, a cow elk is in estrus for 24 hours," Schearer points out. "If she isn't with a bull at that time, she is very excited to get with one and be bred. She makes a series of rapid, excited sounds at this time, sounds that are really quite different from standard cow tones. The excited-cow call can bring bulls on a dead run, and often bring in bulls that have been hesitant to come to more passive cow talk."

COMMON CALLING MISTAKES

"The biggest mistake people make is trying to use cow calls to sound like an elk herd," Schearer says. "The elk you're hunting have lived in the area a long time, and they know that in their roaming they have not missed an entire herd of other elk. But they may have missed a single cow or two, which is why the softer cow calling is a better technique."

On public land, where hunting pressure is high, Schearer will modify his calling. "If there's been a lot of pressure, I will *not* use the 'classic' bugle, but instead use squeals, grunts, and groans. I try to sound like elk without sounding like the typical elk caller/hunter that these animals have been avoiding for days or weeks."

When calling, Schearer cautions that if you make a mistake during the bugling sequence, don't abruptly stop. "Try to salvage the sequence with some grunting or other noise. Remember that elk do not make perfect sounds, either. I also find that bulls start to lose their voices later in the season, thanks to all the bugling and grunting they have done. Their tones change, and they are less likely to make those beautiful, classic scale-type sequences."

Another common mistake is trying to call too often. "It is important to make that bull come and find you," Schearer says. "For example, when locating elk, I'll bugle, then wait quietly for 15 minutes. If I don't hear anything I'll move 500 to 1000 yards, set up, and try again. Don't just bugle, bugle, bugle. Using a stick-and-move pattern is better because it is a more natural sound. A bull won't bugle steadily, and often they are moving when they bugle. Don't bugle just to hear yourself bugle."

When hiking and calling, it is important to be aware of bedded bulls, especially during midday, from about 10:00 A.M. until 3:00 P.M. "During the middle of the day, you'll sometimes hear a bull bugling every 30 minutes or so, but he won't come in to your calling," Schearer says. "That's usually a bull that has bedded down for the day. Now you need to stalk in as close as you can, always being aware of cows and roaming satellite bulls. Get within 150 to 200 yards of the bull, and cow call, trying to get him to come check you out. Stay sharp! Many times satellite bulls will come in silently, so once you blow your elk call, you have to be ready for an elk to come in. Stay patient. Don't call and wait just 15 minutes, then say there are no elk. Wait 20 to 30 minutes before you move after calling. And when you do move, travel slowly and remain on red alert."

What about when the elk simply aren't bugling? "If the weather's hot, or there's a full moon, a lot of times people think the elk aren't in rut, the rut's late, or whatever," Schearer says. "But they really are; they just may be doing most of it at night. Studies have shown that cows drop their calves about the same time each year, so that means they are rutting about the same time, too. In my guide area in Montana, for example, the rut peaks between September 10 and 30.

"To get around this, I make sure I get out at night and listen for elk. I'll often get up from midnight to 1:00 A.M., then again from 4:00 to 5:00 A.M., to try and locate a bull that's been bugling at night. I don't call myself, just listen. If I know where he is, I can try to leave camp extra early and be on him right at first light. Of course, when you hunt this way, you have to sleep some during midday so you can keep at it all week long."

In hot weather, Schearer also recommends setting up by a wallow and cow calling. "Bulls will use wallows heavily during hot weather, and often bed down close to them. Setting a tree stand now is very effective, if you have the patience."

Another mistake novice elk hunters make is overcalling to a hot bull. "If you have a bull that's hot and coming in hard, quit calling and let him keep coming," Schearer suggests. "Make him look for you. If you overcall, he'll see you move for sure. You want him to get close and then have to move around a little to try to find that other elk. That's when he'll present a shot opportunity."

LITTLE THINGS

Schearer always carries a cow call, no matter the season or time of year. If he is still-hunting and not hearing any bugling, he will blow his cow call every 100 yards or so. "I do this in case I break a

The terrain will dictate how often you call, but Schearer believes in calling more often in thick, brushy, or broken ground, which can absorb much of your call's volume.

branch, kick over a rock, or make some other noise. Elk are generally noisy when they walk through the woods, and as long as they don't hear human sounds like voices or metal clanging, they might think you're just more elk cruising the timber."

Schearer likes to sneak up to a ridgeline inside the timber, then peek over to see what's on the other side. "Lots of times bulls will bed just over the top of a ridge, so anytime I crest a ridge I peek over, use my binoculars, and try to find a piece of elk, like an antler tip, ear, rump patch, or leg. I also use my nose. Elk have a distinctive barnyard smell, and many times I've smelled them in the timber before I've seen them." When he sees or smells elk in the timber, Schearer will set up and cow call, hoping the bull will stand up and investigate.

Calling can be difficult on windy days, when sounds don't travel well and it is hard to hear. Then you have to hunt in areas where you *can* hear, at least a little bit. "Get somewhere that is protected from the wind," Schearer suggests. "The lee sides of hills, little hollows and cuts, places like that. Otherwise you'll never hear a bull respond to you unless he is right on top of you."

When hunting with a buddy, make sure that person is standing at least 10 to 15 yards away from you when you blow a locator bugle. "If your hunting buddy is right next to you, the sound of your call will drown out his ability to hear, making it tough for him to detect a distant answer," Schearer says. "An elk may also answer you in the middle of your bugle and you won't be able to hear it, but your buddy may be able to pinpoint the sound." Schearer also recommends calling away from stream noises and such, which can also make it tough to hear a response.

Another key to successfully calling elk is to not get frustrated. "If you are seeing elk sign, the elk are there, and you should always be ready for one to come in to your calling," Schearer says. "Many times, people who have been hunting for days without seeing or

Using the buddy system, with the caller set up 50 to 75 yards behind the shooter, is perhaps the most effective way to get a shot at a bull coming to your calling.

hearing anything will let down their guard. Naturally, that's when a bull will come in quickly and catch them off-guard, and they'll blow their chance.

"You've done your homework, so you know you are hunting a good area," Schearer says. "You have practiced your calling and are making quality elk sounds. By staying at it and not giving up, you are going to get a bull to come in. It's just a matter of time."

7

SNEAK 'EM, DON'T CALL 'EM (with *Randy Ulmer*)

Arizonan Randy Ulmer has been one of the world's most successful competitive archers for more than a decade. He's a pro staff member for several prominent archery companies, including Hoyt USA, Easton Technical Products, Golden Key-Futura, BCY, and Toxonics. On top of that, Randy is a superb bowhunter who has taken an impressive number of giant bulls. His approach to hunting rutting bulls is somewhat different from the textbook "call-'em-in" style. Instead, Randy believes that stealth, speed, and silence are the keys to killing the biggest bull in the woods. Here's how he does it.

In addition to being one of the world's most successful competitive archers, Randy Ulmer is also one of the West's top elk hunters. Although his approach to hunting rutting bulls is different than most hunters, it has been quite effective.

"**E**lk hunting is harder work, physically, than any other type of hunting in North America, except maybe sheep hunting," says Ulmer. "Because elk are 'pocket' animals and the herds move a lot, you have to be able to cover a lot of ground to be able to find animals to hunt. The more miles you can cover in a day or week, the better your chances of success. My system of hunting is based on the ability to travel light and fast until I locate a herd of elk with the type of large, old bull I am interested in, then being able to stay with them until I can get into position for a shot."

KEEP IT SIMPLE

One thing Ulmer has learned over the years is the importance of keeping his equipment simple. This does two things. One, it greatly reduces the chances of anything breaking at the wrong moment. And two, it reduces the amount of weight and bulk he has to carry with him all day, making it easier for him to cover lots of ground and move rapidly when the situation calls for it.

"Keep everything simple when elk hunting," Ulmer advises. "Use things you know will work. An elk hunt is *not* the time to be field testing a new gadget. I like to be able to throw my bow on the ground and know it will still shoot straight and true. For bowhunters, there are a lot of gadgets out there that will help you shoot better on a target or 3-D range but aren't designed to withstand the rough-and-tumble banging they will get on an elk hunt. Your gear *must* be able to take this type of abuse, because you are going to fall down, drop stuff, beat it against trees and rocks, and who knows what else if you are hunting hard. This goes for your weapon as well as your accessories, ancillary hunting equipment, camping gear . . . everything.

"Unlike most elk hunters, who carry a large daypack with a liter of water, lots of food, and 10 pounds of other gear, I do not carry a pack when I am hunting during the day," Ulmer says. "I do not want *any* extra weight weighing me down. There are reasons I can do this. For one thing, I generally hunt in the Southwest during the early archery seasons, where the weather is either mild or downright hot. I'm not worried about being snowed or rained on, or getting hypothermic. Also, there are lots of roads, so I can always get back to camp or my truck and grab some food or water. Sure, I may get a little hungry or thirsty during the day, but the trade-off of a small amount of discomfort for the lack of weight and bulk is worth it to me. In my style of hunting, mobility is the key. I have to be able travel quickly and quietly to get into position to make my move on the herd, and I don't want anything slowing me down when it is time to go fast. I have the necessities at my campsite, including some spare gear and lots of food and drink."

One thing Ulmer has done over the years is keep his equipment simple when hunting elk. Today he does not even carry a daypack with him, believing the added weight will slow him down and not allow him to cover the country and chase after elk the way he needs to.

THE RIGHT CLOTHING

Because Ulmer hunts primarily in arid country during warm or hot weather, he wears cotton chamois outerwear almost 100 percent of the time. "A long-sleeved T-shirt and six-pocket pants are my basic outerwear," he says. "If it's chilly in the morning I may add a light shirt or jacket, but I try not to so I don't have to lug anything extra in the heat of the day. I also wear running shoes instead of boots, because of their light weight and the fact that I actually run a lot to try to get around elk herds. These animals tend to move a long way from bedding to feeding grounds. If you get behind them and try to hunt them from behind, it usually does not work. Instead, I take off and try to circle around and intercept them. The light clothing and running shoes, plus the lack of a daypack filled with 'stuff' I probably won't need, allow me to do this."

In the pockets of his pants, Ulmer carries a pair of camouflage cotton gloves, a camo face net, a small 1-ounce hunting knife, and a latex diaphragm call he uses as a cow call if he needs to stop a bull for a shot. Tucked into the back of his pants are a pair of Bear's Feet or Safari Stalker overshoes. These thick fleece overshoes can be slipped over running shoes, and greatly reduce noise when Ulmer is making a final stalk. He also carries a pair of compact binoculars. "I don't have a spare anything," he says. "I have really cut down over the years, and even though every now and then you get stuck in a small bind, it usually isn't that big a deal. Going all day without water and food, you aren't going to die. I know the country I hunt well, and know what I can get away with. I might have to endure a little hardship, but it isn't all that bad. You look at most guys in the elk woods, and they are so heavy with gear that they can't move quickly or quietly enough to get in position. I can't stress the importance of this enough."

SMELL NO EVIL

One of the biggest changes Ulmer has made over the past decade is the control of his scent.

"Over the years, I have become a scent-control fanatic," he says. "What I found when I first started elk hunting was that 90 percent of the time that elk busted me, it was because they smelled me. I have also found that while you can't do jumping jacks and sing the national anthem in the elk woods and get away with it, elk aren't that sensitive to movement or sound. They travel in herds, and herds make a lot of noise and movement. However, they are *extremely* sensitive to scent. One small whiff of man-smell and they will be out of there!

Ulmer is a scent-control fanatic, employing the same tactics used by tree-stand whitetail hunters—washing clothes in unscented detergent, bathing every day, and using the complete Scent Shield system. "It's amazing the difference this had made in my success," he said.

"My way of hunting has evolved. When I first started elk hunting I would wear the same clothes for a week, and maybe take a bath once a week. Now I bathe at least once a day, even if that means using cold creek or pond water. I use the Scent Shield system of unscented soaps and scent-eliminating sprays. I didn't believe in this stuff until I tried it, but I quickly found out what a big difference it makes. It isn't foolproof, but it significantly reduces the *amount* of odor you put out, and that helps. Ten years ago I had elk smell me 150 to 200 yards away; today I have them walk 50 yards downwind of me and not detect me."

To get the full effect of scent-control products, Ulmer says you have to buy into the whole system and be fanatical about it. "I start taking the Hunter's Deodorant Pill a couple weeks before hunting season. In the field I scrub down with Liquid Body Soap and Body

Guard Shampoo, then use Scent Shield Body Shield Gel over every inch of my body, including my hair. You have to be fanatical and use the whole shebang, but it has reduced the number of times I have been winded. I also try to wear clean, fresh clothes that have been laundered in no-scent detergent and stored in a clean plastic garbage bag in camp. All this is a big hassle, but if you do it, you will be amazed at how much of a difference it makes when you sneak in on a herd of elk."

THE IMPORTANCE OF SCOUTING

Ulmer is a big believer in scouting before the season begins. He tries to locate areas where elk are living undisturbed, and also scouts for true monster bulls. If he finds a herd of elk but they don't hold the size bull he's after, he makes a note of it, then moves on in search of the next herd. "If you want to kill a true giant bull, there is no use wasting your time hunting a herd that doesn't have one," he says. "I know that sounds pretty basic, but a lot of hunters searching for the 'bull of the woods' spend too much of their time hunting areas where one simply does not live."

When the season begins, his scouting allows Ulmer to devise a basic plan of attack. "I know where the elk are, what the country is like, and where they are likely to be bedding and feeding. Most guys don't spend enough time scouting—or, because they are from out of state, don't have the time to scout before the season. They end up spending a big chunk of their hunt simply trying to find a herd. Not me. I want to be right on them from the get-go."

WHAT *TYPE* OF HUNT DO YOU WANT?

Once you have found the elk, it is time to decide on the *type* of hunt you want to have and to structure your game plan accordingly.

"The key, of course, is to get into position to take a shot at a bull you'll be happy with," Ulmer says. "Calling elk is great fun and can be pretty effective, especially if you want to shoot a medium-sized, satellite, or young bull. And there's nothing like the excitement of getting into a calling contest with a mature bull elk! However, I also believe that if you want to get serious about killing the oldest bull in the woods—which may or may not have the biggest antlers—calling may be a big mistake.

"Even if you are the best caller in the world, it is generally the younger bulls that come in. Old bulls don't. The big studs come to a certain point, usually somewhere between 70 and 100 yards, and stop. They will not commit to come any closer. At this point they are looking for another elk. If they don't see one, they get very suspicious and simply won't come in. At 7 to 10 years of age, they've seen a lot of elk hunters, and they are not stupid. They will often turn tail and sneak on out of there. I also think the bigger bulls can tell the

One of the big secrets to Ulmer's success is that he never calls to elk, unless he makes a sharp cow sound to stop a bull for a shot. "If you want to hunt the bull of the woods, I believe you have to sneak in and shoot him without making any noise at all."

difference between people calling and elk calling. These old boys are going to sneak in, take a peek, try to get downwind of the caller and smell what's there. Sure, there's always the odd big bull that gets killed by bugling or cow calling, but that's the exception, not the rule."

Ulmer notes that choosing not to call, and instead trying to work the herd and sneak into position for a shot, is much more demanding, not nearly as much fun, and often less productive. "It's just a matter of what you want from your hunt. Do you want a week full of action and excitement, with increased odds for success, or do you want to roll the dice and see if you can shoot the bull of a lifetime? Both are effective elk hunting methods, but they are as different as night and day."

A TWO-SPEED APPROACH

Once he's located a herd of elk and it's time to move in on them, Ulmer uses one of two speeds. "There is very fast and very slow. There are no medium speeds in my elk hunting. When I've spotted a herd and I may have to circle to get ahead of their line of travel, I go as fast as I possibly can go. That can mean jogging for two to four miles. Once I've gotten into position, however, it becomes a slow, meticulous, still-hunt and stalk game. I've found that it is very difficult for most people to switch gears from full-speed to dead stop. You may race like the wind to get into position, then suddenly find yourself right there, close to the elk. When that happens you have to immediately slow to a crawl or risk spooking them.

"What happens is this," Ulmer continues. "In the morning the elk have reached thick brush or their bedding grounds, and they have slowed down. They're a little nervous, looking, listening, and smelling for danger. You now have to stalk them like you would a bedded mule deer buck, which in my mind is the most difficult of all western game animals to stalk and shoot. If you've gotten ahead

TWO-SPEED APPROACH. If you locate moving bulls, or a moving herd, move into high gear to get ahead and/or above their line of travel. Once you're in position, always with the wind in your favor, slow way down and take your time stalking them. If they bed down, you can either stalk them in their beds or, better, settle in and wait for them to get up after they have completed their nap.

of them and the herd is moving past you, it is also a tough deal. The lead cow is always very, very wary. Then the other elk file by, and they are wired, too. The bigger bulls come last. That means you have to beat all these other elk to get your shot.

"So, here's my ideal morning scenario. I've found a big bull and I have watched him and his herd go to bed. Now I have to make a decision. If I think another hunter may stumble by and bump him, I'll go ahead and try to stalk him. This is very hard, though, and I try to avoid this if I can. There are just too many other elk around to make it a high-percentage game. However, if he is in an area where there is little hunting pressure, I will back off, take a little nap and relax. About 4:00 P.M. or so I will get up and move into a spot 150 yards downwind of the bull, and wait. A couple hours before dark the elk will typically get up, stretch, and nibble around. The bull will usually let out a little growl or soft bugle, and once I hear that I know right where he is. I try to be patient, because now is the best

Ulmer uses a "two-speed" approach to elk hunting. "After spotting a herd, I may have to run as fast as I can to get ahead of them and into position," he said. "But once in close, I slow down to a snail's pace or I'll spook them trying to get a shot."

chance to get him. After his lazy day, that bull is usually lazy and relatively unwary.

"At some point before dark the bull will generally rub a tree, and this is when he becomes very vulnerable," Ulmer says. "Normally a bull will rub for 10 to 15 seconds, then stop for two or three minutes, look around, maybe call a little, but not move much. Then he'll rub again, and stop again. This can go on for maybe 30 minutes, and now is when you have to not hesitate and make your move. I try to approach at a quartering or complete butt-at-me angle. When he is rubbing his tree, I run as fast as I can right at him. The second he stops, I stop. When he starts rubbing again, I run again. Before you know it, you can be within good shooting range of him and get your shot off.

"When I run at a rubbing bull, I could care less about spooking off other elk. They may run off past me or off to the sides, but so what? The bull has his eyes closed when he rubs, and the sounds he makes block out the sounds of the other elk scattering. While I try not to spook any elk out of the area, if there are cows or small bulls between me and my target bull, I forget about them and run at my bull as fast as I can. This may sound a little crazy, but I have shot some really big bulls this way."

If he catches up to the elk herd and gets in tight with them in thick cover, this is when Ulmer may use his diaphragm call.

"Big bulls like to get into the thick stuff as quickly as they can in the morning, and that's where you catch up with them. If you can slip in close enough in this type of cover, you can usually get a quick shot opportunity as they pass through the thick brush and small trees. When I see the bull coming I'll draw my bow and wait for him to get into an opening, then I'll blow sharply on my cow call to stop him. The bull will almost always stop, turn, and look right at me. If you are already at full draw, they will often let you release and watch the arrow all the way in, and not jump the string like a deer. However, they'll run if they see you draw, so you have to be ready to shoot when you sound off on your call."

Ulmer's elk hunting style is certainly different, and not for everyone. One look at his collection of monster elk racks, though, and you have to wonder if perhaps he isn't onto something the rest of us need to give a chance.

RANDY ULMER'S TOP 10 TIPS FOR TAKING GIANT BULLS

1) Don't be afraid to sit. Whitetail tactics, like setting a tree stand over a wallow or water hole, can be very effective. Making the elk come to you without moving is a big advantage.

2) Don't be afraid to run. When elk are moving, they can sometimes go four to five miles from a bedding to feeding area, and vice versa. Most people end up chasing the elk from behind, when the best thing to do is to get in front of them before setting up. Run if you have to, to get in front of them. You can rarely make them turn around and come back.

3) Call sparingly or not at all for old bulls. Big bulls have their harems, and they have been around hunters and elk calling all their lives. Even if you're a world champion, they'll probably know the difference between you and "real" elk. They'll come within 70 to 100 yards, but not into bow range. It's better to try sneaking up on them or judiciously using a cow call.

4) Call profusely for young bulls. Younger "satellite" bulls are very susceptible to calling. They're lonely, need cows, and cow calling can be dynamite on them.

5) If you're not seeing fresh elk sign, don't waste your time. Move to a new spot. Elk move a lot, and you have to be mobile and go where they are.

6) Be prepared. You have to be prepared to hunt in bad weather as well as to handle the massive meat care job killing an elk produces.

7) Use the right equipment. That means tailoring everything, from your weapons to your clothing, backpack and camp gear, and so on, to the specific task at hand. If you want to stay out there and hunt hard for a week or more, you need a comfortable camp, enough food, and the right gear, or you'll end up going home.

8) Practice, practice, practice with your weapon. Make sure you can make the shot under difficult field conditions.

9) Get in shape. Elk hunting on your own is as tough physically as any type of hunting in North America. You can't be in too good shape to hunt elk.

10) Be persistent. A "never-say-die" attitude is the number-one reason for being consistently successful when hunting elk. Also, you have to be mentally tough. Don't get discouraged and quit. Hunt every day as if it is the first day of your hunt.

8

BOWHUNTING BASICS

O ver the past three decades, I've had plenty of memorable encounters with elk. Most of them have come while bowhunting.

Bowhunting is an intimate sport. You have to get up close and personal with game before you can take a good shot, a situation that lends itself nicely to mistakes. The closer an animal gets to you and the longer you take to make a shot, the more chances there are for something to go wrong. A swirl of breeze, a snapped twig, a glare of light, the animal's sixth sense, 1001 other "gotchas"—they all add up to the score usually being elk one, Bob zero.

That's actually the enticement of the sport. I have a saying about big-game hunting that goes something like this: "When the hunt's over with a rifle, it's just beginning with a bow." Roughly

Bowhunting elk is one of the most challenging, yet rewarding, hunting pursuits in all of North America. It takes lots of hard work, dedication, and planning to make your bowhunting dream come true. Mine did on this 1999 hunt.

translated, that means if I see an elk I want and I'm rifle hunting, it's mine. But finding elk when bowhunting is just the start of the game. Seeing elk inside comfortable rifle range means nothing. Getting within 35 yards means everything, and then there are so many other factors to consider. The animal has to be calm and positioned properly, there must be no twigs or brush in the path of the arrow, the sun should be at your back, the wind in your face—you get the picture. For those who are considering taking up the sport, it's important to keep in mind that you'll do a heckuva lot more hunting, and a whole lot less shooting, than you ever did with a firearm.

That's not to say that you can't kill elk with a bow, of course. Thousands of bowhunters do it every year. You can do it, too.

The key word is "dedication." Successful bowhunters are serious about their sport. They take the time to keep their equipment tuned, they practice shooting regularly, they study both their quarry and the area in which they'll be hunting, and they are prepared to hunt hard for several days, or weeks, if necessary. "Persistent" is a word that comes to mind when I think of my most successful bowhunting friends.

BOWS FOR ELK

Despite the fact that they are members of the deer family, in terms of bowhunting *Cervus* really aren't large deer at all—they're the real thing, a *big* game animal. Compared to deer, they have huge, heavily muscled bodies, with bones like iron pipes, shoulder blades like tank armor, and an inherent toughness that makes them a real challenge for a hunter using any type of weapon. For a bowhunter who must get close before shooting, a big bull elk can be intimidating indeed.

What kind of bow should you shoot? Some excellent bowhunters, like my friends Larry D. Jones and Mike Lapinski, successfully hunt elk with their recurves. To them I say, "Congratulations." To you, I say use a compound bow.

Why? Because when an elk comes in close and the brush is thick, you may have to come to full draw and hold it for an extended period of time as you wait for the bull to step out and present a decent shot. It's much easier to hold a compound bow that has wheels and cables to help you at full draw than a recurve, where the only help you'll get is from your shoulder muscles. Becoming proficient with a modern compound bow is much easier than learning to shoot a recurve well. And you can make killing shots at much longer distances with a compound bow.

What kind of compound bow should you use? The best elk bow for you to use is one you're comfortable with and can shoot well. Generally speaking, you need a bow that you can draw smoothly and hold for an extended period of time, in case your bull stops with brush or branches obscuring his chest. They do this a lot! You'll also be ahead of the game if you are able to draw and shoot from your knees, or with your body twisted at an odd angle. And remember that shots can be on the long side, too. The first bull I shot with a bow was taken at 16 yards, while my longest shot—which brought down a large 5×5 bull—was exactly 50 yards. It was the only shot I had in a week of hard hunting. It will greatly benefit you to meticulously tune your bow-and-arrow setup, then extend your maximum shooting range prior to elk season.

Both single- and two-cam compound bows are excellent choices for elk hunting. Many industry experts who are also experienced elk bowhunters recommend a minimum draw weight of 60 pounds for men, and 50 pounds for women, for an elk-hunting bow. Because of the increased efficiency of today's bows, pulling Herculean draw weights isn't necessary to achieve relatively high arrow speed anymore. Companies like Browning, Bear/Jennings, Custom Shooting Systems, Darton, High Country Archery, Hoyt, McPherson Archery, Mathews Archery, Martin, Oneida, and PSE, among others, all build quality bows suitable for elk hunting.

ARROW SHAFTS AND BROADHEADS

Both aluminum and carbon shafts—pure carbon as well as aluminum/carbon composite (A/C/C)—make excellent elk hunting arrows. While I've shot several elk with aluminum arrows, I prefer hunting with pure carbon shafts. I believe they are tougher and penetrate better than comparable aluminum shafts do. That 50-yard bull I described earlier was taken with a carbon shaft, which blew right through his chest and landed a good 20 yards on the other side. The bottom line is matching your shaft to your bow, and shooting a shaft with which you're comfortable and accurate.

Elk have thick chests, heavy hides, and big bones, all good reasons to use quality broadheads with blades so sharp they scare you. I

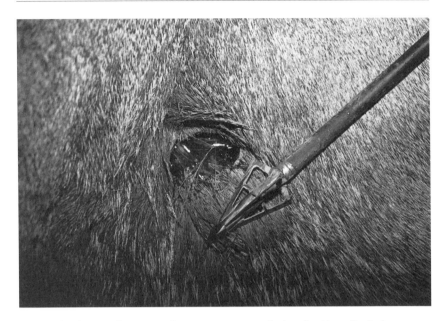

Penetration is more important than raw arrow speed when hunting elk at close range. Razor-sharp broadheads with strong ferrules and thick blades are the preferred choice. I shot this Rocky Mountain Ti-125 clean through a big bull at 40 yards.

prefer 125-grain replaceable-blade heads from companies such as Barrie Archery, New Archery Products, Golden Key-Futura, Muzzy, Sullivan Industries, Game Tracker, AHT, and Archer's Ammo. If you want fixed-blade heads, you can't go wrong with heads from companies like Elk Mountain Archery, Zwickey, Delta, and Magnus. The key is a super-strong ferrule, like Barrie's titanium version, and strong blades. Some excellent elk hunters I know use mechanical broadheads from companies like Barrie Archery, Mar-Den, Sonoran Bowhunting Products, Game Tracker, and New Archery Products.

BOW SIGHTS

Your bow sight needs to be able to withstand some rough field abuse. Fiber-optic bow sight pins are ideal, as elk are often taken

deep inside the dark timber or on the cusp of daylight. Make sure
your sight has a rugged pin guard, a minimum of moving parts that
can rattle loose, and can be secured tightly to the bow's riser. Sights
from companies like Sonoran Bowhunting Products, TruGlo, Sight
Master, Fine-Line, Browning, PSE, Jennings Archery, Cobra, Toxonics, and Montana Black Gold are examples of good sights for elk
hunting. If you use a peep sight, get one that lets in maximum avail-

*Fiber-optic bow sights permit you to see your pins clearly at dawn and dusk, when elk are
most active, as well as in the dark timber, where they spend most of their time.*

able light. Fine-Line's Sta-Brite, Game Tracker's Dusk Vision, the Shepley Peep, Cee-Peep, and Shurz-A-Peep are all good.

ACCESSORIES

In terms of bow accessories, keep it simple. This is especially true when hunting elk in the western mountains, where you're often a day or more's trip to the nearest archery shop.

In my mind, a bow-attached quiver is the way to go for all western hunting. Your arrows are conveniently at hand, and you won't have to worry about clanging and banging shafts noisily against brush, as you will when wearing a hip quiver.

I prefer wrist strap-type release aids, primarily because the strap keeps them from falling off when I'm moving quickly to get into position for a shot. There are many excellent releases out there. Those from Pro Release, Scott Archery, Golden Key-Futura, Jim Fletcher Archery, Tru-Fire, Winn Archery, Jerry Carter, and T.R.U. Ball are all excellent.

Arrow rests can be a source of frustration if you don't get a good one. Choose a rest with few moving parts or screws, and which can be adjusted easily. Golden Key-Futura, New Archery Products, Savage Systems, and Bodoodle all make hunting rests that fit these criteria.

I also find it advantageous to carry a couple of shafts tipped with either Judo or Bludgeon points, which I use for stump-shooting practice. A laser range finder, like the Bushnell Yardage Pro Compact 600, can be a huge help in determining the exact distance to the target over the often deceptive western terrain. And something that makes it easy to constantly check the wind, like Knight & Hale's Windfloaters, a butane lighter, or a small puff bottle filled with unscented talc, carpenter's chalk, or cornstarch, is essential. Unless you can beat the wind, and with it an elk's radar nose, you'll never get the chance to shoot a single arrow.

Your bow should have string silencers and be painted a camouflage or dark color, with all shiny parts dulled or painted to avoid game-spooking glare. Pad the arrow shelf and underside of your sight pin guard with felt or electrician's tape so arrows won't clank against bare metal if they accidentally fall off the arrow rest. It's also important to have basic tools and a simple assortment of parts like extra nock points, peep sight, sight pins, bowstring release, and so on in camp, just in case.

PRACTICE: THE KEY TO SUCCESS

The best elk setup you can carry into the woods is the one you shoot well and have unblinking confidence in. This confidence is developed through practice—lots of it.

Practice as often as you can. Shooting on the target range is always helpful, and I make sure I do lots of it all year. This helps me

Practice is the key to bowhunting success. Though most shots at elk will be under 20 yards, I have shot bulls at twice that distance. It pays to be prepared.

make sure my shooting form is correct, that my bow is sighted in, and that everything works. Better still is practice on targets set at unknown distances. Participating in 3-D animal target shoots is another excellent way to practice. Here you shoot at actual three-dimensional animal targets set at different distances. Archery shops are good places to find out about these shoots.

I'm constantly practicing while elk hunting, too. I carry plenty of blunts, and shoot at rotten stumps, grass clumps, dirt clods, pinecones, and other inanimate objects all day long. This gives me a feel for the country, and helps sharpen my range-estimation eye. I also always carry a range finder; using it as I hike along helps me verify my guesses as to how far away a tree, rock, or stump might be. Misjudging range in the field, especially when the quarry is a deceptively large elk, is easy to do. It's also important to practice shooting at steep up-and-down angles. Elk country is rarely level, and shots at bull above or below you are the rule, not the exception. You need to know where your arrow will hit at a given distance when shooting up and down. Only practice will tell you.

Practice will also tell you how far you can shoot accurately. It's critical to know your limitations, and to not take shots you can't make every time. Most shots at elk will be between 15 and 30 yards, though if you can shoot accurately out to 40 yards you'll be better off. I have a 50-yard pin on my bow, and won't hesitate to shoot at that distance if everything is perfect: the elk calmly standing broadside and unaware of my presence, and me having time to use my range finder to determine the exact distance to the target.

CAMOUFLAGE, CLOTHING, AND SCENT

Elk have excellent eyesight when it comes to detecting movement and the obvious out-of-place object in the woods. For that reason, it's wise to wear camouflage when bowhunting elk.

Total camouflage is the way to go. Don't overlook your face, neck, and hands. I either use face paint on the neck and face or wear a light camouflage head net with eye holes. My shooting gloves are also camouflage.

Only soft, nonabrasive fabrics like wool, fleece, or well-softened cotton are acceptable. Denim, nylon, and the like will scratch against brush and trees, making sounds guaranteed to spook elk. Crepe-soled boots or lightweight running shoe-type footwear is also preferable to hard-soled lug bottoms, for the same reason. Tape over metal belt buckles and other exposed hard surfaces on your clothing, to keep them from glinting in the sunlight and ringing against brush.

Just as important as wearing total camouflage is movement. Don't underestimate an elk's keen eyesight, even in timber. Elk can detect the slightest movement in the woods, and will stare it down until they determine what it is. If an elk sees you move, it will often stop, stare, and wait for you to move again so it can positively identify you. If you don't move again it may forget about you, but it will probably spook. It's best not to let them see you move at all.

The elk's primary defense is its nose. Once an elk gets a whiff of you, it's "Sayonara!" If you don't get the wind in your favor, you'll never get a bow shot at an elk. Always hunt with the wind in your face. If you're in a calling contest with a bull and the wind is swirling or unsteady, it's wise to back off and wait for it to steady up. This is true even if it means leaving the bull alone for the rest of the day and trying him tomorrow. True, he may not be there tomorrow. But then again he might, and conditions might be more in your favor. If you try him in uneven wind and he smells you, he'll be out of your life forever. Count on it.

Modern scent-eliminating products can help you when elk hunting, just as they can when tree stand whitetail hunting. To be effective, you have to be meticulous and consistent in their use. For more on this aspect, see Chapter 7, "Sneak 'Em, Don't Call 'Em."

Watching every little puff of breeze is critical when you're in tight to a herd of elk. Using a wind-detection device, like the Knight & Hale Windfloater, is a big help.

THE SETUP

Most bowhunters will get their shots at elk by either calling them in or ambushing them as they move by. In either case, having a good setup is the difference between merely seeing elk up close and getting a high-percentage shot. After all, if all I wanted to do was look at elk up close, I'd go to Yellowstone Park or the zoo.

Always set up in the shade or shadows, with a dark background behind you to keep from being silhouetted. You need something to break up your outline—brush, sticks, tree limbs, and so on. You also need shooting lanes, open areas that will give you an unimpeded shot when the elk gets close. Ideally, you need a shooting lane to each side and one in front.

You also need barriers in front of you that will make the elk come broadside to you when he comes into bow range. If you don't

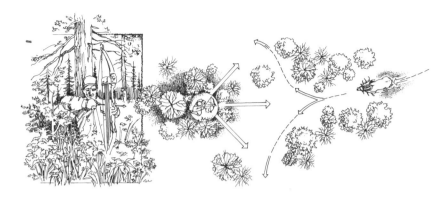

AMBUSH SPOT. Find a spot in the shade or in shadows, with a dark background to keep you from being silhouetted. You'll need something to break up your outline, such as brush, sticks, or tree limbs. You'll also need shooting lanes that give you unimpeded shots in front and to the sides. Barriers in front of you, to make the elk come broadside to you when he gets within bow range, complete your ambush point.

have a barrier set up and the elk comes to a call, he may walk straight in, giving you no shot at all. Ideally these barriers are also something the elk can walk behind, hiding his eyes from you as you come to full draw. *Never* draw the bow when an elk can see you. If you do, he'll be gone so fast it will make your head spin. If the bull is

The set-up is everything in bowhunting. You have to be in the shade with an outline-breaking background, and have open shooting lanes to all sides. You'll often be shooting from your knees or some kind of awkward position.

walking broadside to you within bow range, let him walk past so you're out of his direct line of sight before drawing. This slight quartering-away angle presents an excellent shot.

I try to make the elk walk to me up the slope. I feel this gives me a big advantage, both in getting a good shot and having the flexibility to move quickly and stay with the elk should I have to change position.

WHAT'S A GOOD SHOT?

There are really only two good shots. The best is when the bull is completely broadside to you, yet in such a position that you can draw and shoot without its seeing you. The other is if the elk is quartering slightly away. Both angles will give you an open path to put your arrow through the lungs, the best hit you can get.

Elk quartering toward you, facing you directly, or facing away from you have too much bone, muscle, and hide for the arrow to penetrate through to the lungs. Don't take these shots, no matter how tempting they may be.

The same rules apply if you're in a tree stand. It's important to hit the elk in both lungs, not just one. I've seen bulls punched through only one lung run a very long way before being recovered. I'm talking miles here, not hundreds of yards. A double-lung hit, on the other hand, means a quick death. And that's what you want. Every time.

AFTER THE SHOT

Okay, so your dreams have been realized. A big bull elk came into your coaxing cow call, and you got a good shot. You think the hit was good, but you're not sure. Now what do you do?

Relax.

That's much easier said than done. Nothing gets the adrenaline pumping through my veins faster than calling an elk in close, then shooting him with my bow. Once you have made your shot, stay calm as the elk runs off. Give a soft cow call or two. Confused about what's happening, the elk may stop at the sound of the cow call, even if it's been shot through the chest. I once saw a big, rut-crazed bull shot through both lungs stop immediately at the sound of a cow call, stand listening for the other elk while his time ran out, and then drop dead in his tracks. Even if you miss, a cow call may calm the elk down. I've seen missed bulls come back in and give the shooter—me—another chance, thanks to the cow call.

When the elk finally runs off, replay the scene in your mind. Was the hit good? Bad? A miss? Wait a full 30 to 60 minutes, sitting as quietly as your shaking hands will let you. If it's starting to rain or snow, you'll have to make a judgment call on whether or not to act immediately. When you do move, go to the spot where the elk was standing when you shot and look for both blood and your arrow. But do so quietly—no talking, whooping and hollering, or unnecessary noise. If the elk has bedded down close by, you want him to stay there. Hearing you will make him run farther away, making recovery even more difficult.

The arrow shaft will tell you many things about the hit. Foamy red blood indicates a lung hit, deep red blood with no froth a liver or heart hit, while greenish food particles in the blood indicate a paunch hit. Lung, liver, and heart shots should do the elk in quickly; quietly follow them up right away. On a paunch hit, wait at least half a day, weather permitting, to allow the bull to bed down, stiffen up, and expire without really knowing what happened. If the shot came in the evening, wait until morning to begin the search.

Don't be surprised if the blood trail is a scant one, even if the hit was solid in the heart/lung area. Big elk often leave blood trails similar to those of deer—just a spot of blood every now and then. The bleeding is taking place internally, and the hide, hair, and body fat are keeping it from flowing out. You may have to follow the trail on hands and knees, backtracking and trying to figure out just where your elk went. Mark the trail with fluorescent-orange flagging so you

After the shot, remain quiet, relax, and try to find your arrow. The blood on the shaft will tell you where you hit your bull.

Bowhunters have the advantage of being able to hunt during the rut, when most rifle seasons are closed. My big New Mexico bull came to a cow call; he scored 344 6/8 Pope & Young points.

won't lose it. (Just make sure to pick up all your flagging when you're done.)

I once tracked a bow-shot elk for six hours, backtracking and redefining the trail with tiny irregular blood spots, hoof prints, and intuition. I shot the bull at 9:30 A.M. and finally found him at 4:00 P.M. The hit had been perfect, through both lungs, and the bull hadn't traveled a quarter mile. But the terrain was steep and rocky, the bull didn't bleed much at all, and he didn't leave many tracks. It was a tough trailing job that demanded persistence.

But when I found that bull, the feeling was one of total elation. Once you experience that same feeling, you'll be hooked for life. That's what bowhunting elk is all about.

9

HUNTING THE GENERAL RIFLE SEASON
(with *George Taulman*)

One of the best elk hunters I've had the privilege of hunting with over the years is George Taulman, head of United States Outfitters (USO). Taulman became a full-time outfitter in the late 1980s; since then he has built USO into the largest elk outfitter in the country, with hunting operations in several states. Taulman also runs the USO Professional Licensing Service, the first western licensing service, where, for a nominal fee, his staff will do the research for you, then apply you for the best western hunts for whatever species you're interested in, including elk. If you don't draw the hunt you're dreaming of one year and choose to do so, Taulman will continue applying you for the same hunt year after year, helping you accumulate the bonus points you need to finally pick the tag. If you draw a tag while using his licensing service, you are not obligated to hunt with his guides, but are free to hunt on your own if you wish.

George Taulman heads up United States Outfitters, the West's largest and most successful elk guiding business. His experiences during the general rifle season shed a unique light on how to tip the odds in your favor.

Taulman's experiences have given him what would be the equivalent of a Ph.D. in elk hunting. His insights on elk hunting, and elk behavior, during the general rifle season will help you understand where to find bulls that often seem to disappear moments after opening morning. For more information on his guided hunts and licensing service, contact USO at P.O. Box 4204, Taos, NM 87571; 1-800/845-9929.

"The general rifle season is really the toughest time of the year to kill a bull," says Taulman. "In most states the seasons open after the rut has peaked, and most of the bigger bulls just want to be left alone. The weather can be anything from hot to rainy to cold and snowy, so you have to be prepared for anything and everything.

"The good bulls usually want to rest and recover from the rut, and they'll head for the steepest, nastiest dark timber patches in an area, including the higher timbered basins. They'll stay in these areas until the heavy snows force them out and down onto their winter range."

THE IMPORTANCE OF SCOUTING

Taulman definitely recommends scouting your hunting area prior to the start of your hunt. "It's very important not just that you locate some elk, but also that you get an idea of the terrain so you can anticipate where the animals will go once the shooting starts. When you begin to think like an elk as well as a hunter, your chances of filling your tag will go way up."

According to Taulman, one of the mistakes that many hunters make is that they want to sit and glass open parks and meadows. "Elk do like these places because of the high-quality grass that grows in the open sunlight. However, hunting pressure has changed their habits. Now they feed in these parks primarily at night, usually leaving them before daylight and entering right at dusk, or just after dark. You'll still see beds, droppings, and tracks in the parks, but as

Scouting is the key to a successful elk hunt regardless of season. Who would not want to hunt the bull that made these monster tracks?

the saying goes, the only track I want to see is one with an elk standing in it.

"I find that elk like to bed on north- and east-facing slopes, where the foliage is thickest and the temperature coolest. Most north slopes are spruce, fir, and the like, while on south slopes you'll find more lodgepole pine and a more open, drier climate. The lushest grass is usually on the south and west slopes, which is where the elk prefer to feed. There are exceptions, of course, but these are general rules."

When scouting, you need to find as many herds of elk as you can. This way, if your hunt for a bull from herd A fails, you have a backup plan that you can turn to immediately—herd B. It's also important to anticipate the actions of other hunters, and plan accordingly. You have to assume that your elk are going to be bumped by other hunters. Where will they go? Where will they bed? Ask yourself these questions before opening day, and you'll be ahead of the game.

It's also important to consider the wind when rifle hunting for elk. Many hunters believe the wind is only important in bowhunting, when you have to get close, but that isn't so. "I've had elk smell me at over 300 yards away, and turn and leave the area for good," Taulman says. "If an elk sees you, it's bad news, but sometimes you can get away with it. If they smell you, it's all over. When scouting, pay attention to the prevailing wind conditions."

MAKE A PLAN

Smart hunters enter the mountains with some sort of game plan based on their research, scouting, and experience.

"Let's say it's opening morning. I've scouted the area and either seen elk or found some fresh sign that tells me there are elk living in the area," Taulman says. "I may dream that I'm the only hunter in the state who has seen these elk, but in reality, other groups of hunters probably have, too. If I'm hunting in an area where there will be some hunting pressure opening morning, I'll try to anticipate that pressure. Instead of going to the elk right off the bat, I may instead go to their escape route and set up. These are usually saddles, timber patches, timbered fingers, and the tops of timbered ridges. This way, when other hunters bump the elk, I'm in an excellent position to get a shot. And if by chance no one does spook my elk, I can go back and hunt them later on.

"It's also been my experience that spooked elk will usually go up, not down," Taulman notes. "For this reason, the hunter should do whatever it takes to get high and into position before first light. In the steep elk mountains, it's much easier physically for us to hunt down than it is up. If you try chasing elk up the mountain, you're wasting your time. There's no way you can physically catch them."

Taulman is a proponent of the "pocket principle," a theory that says that while the available range may all be ideal for elk to live in, only a small part of it will hold elk at any given time. "You need to

OPENING MORNING. In areas with hunting pressure, go high early in the morning, and set up overlooking elk escape routes. Look for saddles, timber patches, timbered fingers, and the tops of timbered ridges. Take a stand where the wind is blowing in your favor, and where you can overlook more than one trail. When elk head up the mountain, in front of hunters moving up from down below, you'll be ready.

realize that elk are herd animals, and live in isolated pockets within their range. Even in the best elk country, where elk numbers are high, only a small portion of the range will hold the animals at any given time. For that reason, you need to hunt reasonably quickly until you find fresh sign. Then, slow down and work the area thoroughly before moving on. This 'fast trolling' method will keep you from wasting lots of time in areas that may look good but don't hold any elk."

Taulman likes to hunt feeding areas early and late in the day. "I've found that even if I shoot in a feeding area, I may not spook the elk completely out of the country, though they'll certainly run off. However, if you hunt them in their bedding areas and spook them, they'll usually leave the area for good. Bedding areas are where elk feel they're safe and protected. Show them they're not, and they'll find another, more secure place to live."

SPOT AND STALK SECRETS

The key to consistent success during rifle season is simple: Glass long and hard, and don't be afraid of the dark. You can't be afraid to hike to and from camp in the dark; you want to be glassing as soon as it is light enough to see and in a likely area, glassing until you can't see anymore in the evening.

"Unlike people, deer, elk, and other ungulates have eyes that actually see better in twilight than at other times," Taulman points out. "That's one reason they're most active just before, and just after, it gets barely light enough for us to see, and after dark. Also, once hunting pressure accelerates in a given area, elk are more likely to move and feed at night. In these areas 'prime time' is the first 30 minutes you can see in the morning and the last 30 minutes in the

Taulman likes to hunt feeding meadows in the evenings. Usually, the elk won't leave the timber and enter the meadows until right at dark. You have to be set up and be ready if you're going to catch the bulls outside the dark timber during shooting light.

evening. These are the two times your chances of spotting elk moving in open areas are best."

WHERE AND HOW TO LOOK

"You must be able to look over the maximum amount of country when glassing," Taulman says. "That generally means climbing to a high point overlooking a valley, or a spot that allows you to glass into the timbered pockets on the opposite ridge. As it grays up in the morning, concentrate on open parks and meadows. These areas reflect a lot of available light, making it easy to see into them first. As it gets lighter, if you don't see any elk in these openings, start glassing into the timber, looking for trails, small meadows, and saddles.

"It's important to get comfortable, sit down, and rest your elbows on your knees as you glass. Standing will only cause rapid fatigue, and not let you really 'see' the country. Many people use a

Climbing high and glassing lots of country will help you locate moving elk. The secret is to be on your glassing station well before first light, and again until it is too dark to see.

grid pattern, starting on one side of the area, sweeping their binoculars across it, raising them a bit, then sweeping back. If they don't see anything, they do it again. You have to have both faith in your spot and the patience to continue glassing when no elk appear. Sometimes it pays to move 50 to 100 yards along your ridgetop to give you a different angle.

"During midday, concentrate your glassing efforts into the timber," Taulman concludes. "Look for the shiny bodies of bedded elk along the edges of timber stringers. By glassing across the valley into the timber on the other side, you can sometimes pick up elk as they move around in the trees. This can help you determine where they're bedding and be the first step in planning an ambush or drive."

THE IMPORTANCE OF QUALITY OPTICS

The importance of using only the very best optics you can afford cannot be overstated. Top-quality glass eliminates eyestrain, produces a clear, sharp image even "way out there," and strains every last bit of light out of early dawn and dusk, times when elk are most active. Names such as Bausch & Lomb, Leica, Swarovski, Zeiss, Nikon, and Leupold will never disappoint you, even though they cost a fair chunk of change.

Binoculars in the $7\times$ to $10\times$ range are standard out west. Bring those that can use a lot of light, meaning binoculars with a large objective lens in relation to power. 7×35, 8×30, 8×40, 10×40, and 10×50 binoculars are large and somewhat heavy, but worth every ounce. Spotting scopes with variable eyepieces in the $15-45\times$ and $20-60\times$ class are best, if you choose to pack one.

Glassing should be part of every elk hunter's repertoire. Make sure you're on station at prime time, bring along quality optics, be meticulous in your search, and you'll up your odds for success tenfold.

Quality optics—binoculars as well as rifle scopes—can be critical to the success of your hunt.

MAKE HUNTING PRESSURE WORK *FOR* YOU

What happens when you scout an area, find the elk, and are ready for a great hunt when, just before the opening bell rings, other hunters start arriving in droves? You simply put these newcomers to work for you.

"Here's what you do when that happens—and it happens more than we like to think it does on many public land hunting areas these days," Taulman says. "Instead of sleeping in to the last minute, crawl out of your sleeping bag in the middle of the night, eat a quick breakfast, grab your rifle and daypack, and quietly start up the mountain by flashlight. Keep a low profile, be careful not to let the other camps see or hear you, and climb high. Set up in a saddle high above the valley floor. Pick a spot that overlooks a lot of country, with well-used elk trails coming out of the top of the timber stringers, and leading into your saddle and over the mountain. This

Bob Robb shot this fine 6 × 6 bull during the general rifle season in Montana. By climbing high well before first light, he let other hunters in the area push the elk up to him.

is a natural pathway for the elk to use as an escape route between one drainage and the next.

"Get comfortable, wait patiently, and watch diligently," Taulman suggests. "The chances are good that hunters trying to hunt from the bottom up will drive some elk right past you. This isn't rocket science. You have basically two choices—hunt with the masses and hope for the best, or let the masses work for you, not against you. Recognize the opportunity when it arises. Then, thanks to previous scouting and/or knowledge of the terrain, you can place yourself where the elk are likely to move once they're spooked."

WEATHER PATTERNS AND ELK

Changeable weather is the name of the game during the rifle season. You need to be ready to hunt according to the dictates of Mother Nature, which is not always the way you'd prefer to hunt.

"When the weather is hot and dry, the first glimmer of light in the morning and the last glow of light in the evening are the key times," Taulman explains. "During the day the elk will be bedded in the dark timber, probably near the tops of ridges on the north slopes, where the breeze will cool them down. They may also wallow some during the day.

"On the other end of the spectrum is extremely cold weather. However, what is extremely cold to you and me isn't cold to an elk at all. I've seen them bedded down in the shaded timber when it was zero degrees out, happy as clams and doing their best to avoid the direct sunlight. But once the mercury drops to well below zero, the elk have to eat a lot to stay warm. Then you can find them out and about at odd times. I've seen them out in open meadows feeding as late as 10:00 A.M., and back out as early as 2:00 P.M., when it was 30 degrees below zero."

High winds make elk hunting tough. Because most elk country is made up of uneven terrain, the winds are constantly shifting, making it difficult to hunt effectively. The elk seem spookier than usual, too. If you can wait it out, it's best to just sit and glass during the strong winds. Rain, on the other hand, doesn't seem to affect elk very much. In hot weather, they like its coolness. Hunting in a light rain can be very effective because it quiets the woods, making it easier to slip along undetected. The same is true of a light snow. However, if it's a monsoonlike rain, or blizzardlike snow, the elk will hole up and wait out the storm. When the storm breaks, start hunting hard, as the animals will be up and feeding.

CALLING DURING THE EARLY RIFLE SEASON

Most general rifle seasons open in October, after the rut has peaked. However, there is still a little rutting activity happening through the month and into November, and it isn't that unusual to hear a bull bugle, especially during the early rifle seasons. "I think sometimes the elk bugle just to sound their own horn," Taulman says. "I think it's usually smaller bulls at this time, though. We often locate bulls by bugling, then listening for a response, before moving in on the sounds."

The most effective call now is the cow call, Taulman says. "Elk make cow sounds all year, so you need to be listening for them as you hunt the timber. I like to cow call from time to time as I hunt the dark timber, hoping the elk will think it's one their cousins tromping along, and not some city slicker with a .30–06. I try not to overdo it, though. I'd much rather find elk without making any noise at all."

Cow calls can also help mask your presence, especially if elk see or hear you. You can often calm half-spooked elk with a cow call or two. Like any elk-hunting tool, cow calls are worth carrying, but they're not magic wands that will mystically erase blatant mistakes.

It is possible to call elk to you even during the early and mid-season rifle hunts. A rifle hunter's best friend is his cow call, which can be used to locate elk in thick timber, call them within range, and stop them for a shot.

The general rifle season is one of the toughest times to take a good bull. Careful planning and hard hunting will help tip the odds in your favor. Bob Robb took this New Mexico 6×6 on a general rifle hunt in New Mexico.

HOW MUCH TIME DO YOU NEED?

"Every year, a few lucky hunters shoot a nice bull the first morning of their hunting trip. I've done it before, and so have many of my clients," Taulman says. "But more than likely it's going to take time to fill your elk tag. Lots of it. The toughest thing in the world is to shoot a bull elk on a weekend hunt. Just about the time you're beginning to figure out the country, the elk movement patterns, and so on, it's time to go home. On weekend hunts, it's much better to be lucky than good.

"On a guided hunt, I like to hunt for a minimum of five days. Seven days is better, 10 days better still, and 14 days ideal, especially for a do-it-yourselfer. The more time you can spend in the woods, the better your chances. Also, be realistic in your goals. Don't expect to find a magazine-cover 6×6 bull behind every tree. It just ain't so.

"In reality, any bull elk is a trophy to be proud of. Another funny thing is that many people who have a cow tag think that they can just waltz right out into the woods and shoot a cow whenever they want. Many times bagging a cow is just as tough, or tougher, than shooting a bull elk.

"There are lots of elk in the woods these days, and plenty of good hunting opportunities, something we should all be thankful for," Taulman concludes. "But bagging an elk is still hard work. If you're willing to meet the challenge, the rewards are great."

10

MUZZLELOADER MAGIC
(with Harold Knight & David Hale)

The hunting and game-calling expertise of Harold Knight and David Hale is well known to sportsmen across the country. Knight & Hale Game Calls is one of the most successful businesses of its kind, thanks in no small part to the skill and charisma of Harold and David. In addition to the call business, "Knight & Hale's Ultimate Hunting" cable television show and video series are both highly rated and successful. Harold and David made their first elk hunt more than a decade ago; since then they have become extremely proficient pursuing big bulls with both muzzleloaders and archery tackle. For more information on Knight & Hale game calls, hunting products, and videos, contact the company at Drawer 670, Cadiz, KY 42211; 1-800/500-9357.

Harold Knight is a master at taking big bull elk with a muzzleloader. This giant New Mexico 6 × 6 is just one of the many trophy-class bulls he has taken in recent years.

I n the 1960s and '70s, when states first began offering a few special muzzleloader-only seasons, hunters who chose muzzleloaders were more concerned with nostalgia than "making meat," hoping to step back into time and hunt with the tools of the old trappers and pioneers. I was one of them. At that time, deer numbers—especially eastern whitetails—were nothing like they are today in many parts of the country. With few antlerless seasons, the chances of success on any hunting trip were not good. Many blackpowder hunters of that era resigned themselves to the fact that while they would go home empty-handed, they'd at least be hunting with a tool that brought back memories and helped them live out their wilderness fantasies. State wildlife managers were also more concerned with providing increased hunter opportunity while not significantly increasing the overall deer harvest. For that reason, muzzleloader seasons were quite restrictive.

In sharp contrast, muzzleloading elk hunters of today are for the most part sportsmen and women more concerned with the chance to put a tag on a big bull or fat cow during one of the special muzzleloader-only seasons—especially seasons held during the rut—than with nostalgic ties to yesterday. Most have never even read *The Leatherstocking Tales*, or seen the old Daniel Boone and Davy Crockett TV shows that inspired many traditional muzzleloader shooters. And while some states restrict the use of certain types of muzzleloaders during their blackpowder seasons, the general public for the most part is more concerned with performance than nostalgia. Today, muzzleloading elk hunters have the finest equipment ever offered. It's easy to travel back to the future and become a successful modern muzzleloader elk hunter.

Many muzzleloader-only elk seasons are held at least partially during the rut, when bulls are bugling and excitement runs high. This is the time the savvy hunter can call bulls to him, increasing his odds. The Knight and Hale game-calling team is a huge fan of

David Hale likes to hunt muzzleloader bulls during the rut in southern-tier states, where the weather is warm and the odds are good that he can call a big bull into range of his Knight in-line rifle.

muzzleloader elk hunting, and especially those seasons held during the rut. Over the years they have learned several tricks of the trade that can help you punch your own tag.

WHY MUZZLELOADERS FOR ELK?

"In most states you still have the opportunity to take part in the bugling season, where you cannot anymore with a centerfire rifle," says David Hale. "The advantage is that your 'needle in the haystack' is now a noisy, vocal animal; what I cannot normally see, I can now find by hearing him bugle, and that makes for a good starting place when I'm trying to find a bull to hunt."

"The other key muzzleloader advantage is that even though the bugling season is winding down during most muzzleloader seasons, you do not have to get as close as you do with a bow and arrow," says Harold Knight. "My effective range with the Knight

EARLY MUZZLELOADING. *Early-season muzzleloading gives you opportunities you might not get later in the season. Bulls will be bugling, possibly sparring. Try to pattern a big bull, then get above his territory early in the morning, in a spot where you can glass and call. This might overlook a saddle, bowl, basin, or a patch of isolated timber. Elk generally work their way from low-level feeding areas to higher-elevation bedding areas. The thermal currents are also rising in the morning, so the wind will always be in your favor.*

DISC rifle is between 150 and 200 yards, when I'm hunting in states that permit the use of a scope. When I get a bull to show himself, I can usually shoot him. With a bow, it's a million times tougher."

Hale also noted that some states offer late muzzleloader hunts where you can hunt bulls that are either on or approaching their winter range. "Conditions then can be cold, snowy, wet, and miserable, and the crunchy snows makes sneaking up on them tough," Hale says. "But if you can handle the conditions, these seasons are super times to take a big bull."

MODERN HUNTERS VS. OLD-TIME TRADITIONALISTS

Today, blackpowder hunters have two choices of rifle style—exposed hammer and in-line. Exposed hammer rifles are of the classic design, with a hammer you have to thumb back to cock before firing. They are still popular, and there are some sidehammer rifles available today that rival the more modern in-line style in performance and accuracy.

However, in-line rifles are truly the "back to the future" of muzzleloading. "In-line" refers to the muzzleloader's ignition system, which places the rifle's nipple and percussion cap (or, in some cases, a shotgun primer) in a straight line with the barrel and powder charge. No longer does the spark have to make a sharp turn to find the powder. This, in turn, has improved the reliability of the ignition so much that the hang-fires and misfires that plague more traditional percussion rifles are rare.

Most people don't realize that the in-line design is not a true modern development, but rather an improvement on a basic design that dates back to 1700s-era flintlocks. Theory has it that a lack of springs strong enough to drive the in-line hammers forward fast enough probably kept this design from supplanting sidehammer

Modern in-line muzzleloaders can produce excellent accuracy, even with open sights. This .50-caliber Knight rifle put three Nosler Partition-HG Hunting Sabots into a 3-inch circle at a distance of 100 yards.

firearms. And while there were a few in-lines around in the 1970s and '80s, they never really did catch on with hunters and shooters.

Then along came Tony Knight, a gunsmith from Lancaster, Missouri. Knight (not related to Harold Knight) had customers who traveled to Colorado to hunt the state's muzzleloader-only elk season in the late 1970s and early '80s. Being new to the blackpowder game, they soon found—as many of us did—they had trouble making their reproduction percussion rifles go off when they wanted them to, if they could even haul the long-barreled 9-pound guns up and down the mountains. They took their troubles to Knight, who had a small shop in the garage of the family farm and no muzzleloading experience. Without any preconceived notions, he designed a hunting rifle that just happened to be a muzzleloader. In his eye, hunting rifles had round 22-inch barrels, not three-foot octagonal tubes, weighed less than 8 pounds, and used the practical in-line ignition design.

Knight made his first in-line rifle in 1983. In 1985 he introduced the Knight MK-85, which set the tone for both the industry and the hunters it served. The Modern Muzzleloading, Inc. MK-85 had modern rifle features, including receivers drilled and tapped for scope mounts and adjustable trigger, plus a removable breech plug that greatly simplified cleaning and permitted hunters to push an unfired charge out the breech at day's end, instead of having to either pull the ball or bullet out the barrel or fire the rifle, which meant a half-hour's cleaning session. Other makers like White, Thompson/Center, and CVA soon jumped onto the bandwagon. Today there is a raft of additional companies, like Traditions, Gonic Arms, Markesbery Muzzleloaders, Navy Arms, Dixie Gun Works, and Austen & Halleck, offering top-quality in-line muzzleloaders. Many names most of us associate with centerfire rifles—Remington, Ruger, and Marlin—are also building and selling quality in-line muzzleloaders.

IN-LINE PERFORMANCE

Despite all the hoopla, in-lines are still muzzleloading, blackpowder firearms. To hear many of their detractors, you'd think they provide the ballistic performance of some new souped-up centerfire magnum round. Not so. However, they do provide better ballistic performance than the front-stuffers of old.

For example, my standard elk-hunting load for several of the .50-caliber in-lines I've hunted with (.50 caliber is by far the most popular caliber sold today, followed by .54 caliber) produces about 1475 ft.-lbs. of energy at the muzzle, and retains 1100 ft.-lbs. at 100 yards when using a saboted conical bullet weighing in the 240- to 260-grain class and 100-grain equivalent of Pyrodex Select or two 50-grain Pyrodex Pellets. I can get a bit more energy, but lose a bit of trajectory, by going up to a 300-grain bullet. Still, if I zero these rifles

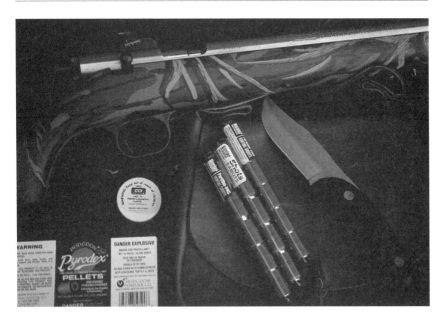

Muzzleloading hunters need several accessories to keep them shooting straight, including either Pyrodex (in both granulated or pellet form), percussion caps, and conical-type bullets.

to print between 2 and 3 inches high at 100 yards—the same way I sight in most of my centerfire rifles—the bullet will strike 3 or 4 inches low at 150 yards. Group size isn't satisfactory to me if I can't produce three-shot, 2-inch clusters at 100 yards.

Many in-lines can top this performance. Present-day rifles from Modern Muzzleloading (Knight), Thompson/Center, and Traditions, among others, are built to accept three 50-grain Pyrodex Pellets. When loaded with a 250-grain sabot-encased bullet, they can produce muzzle velocities of 2100 fps or so. In an advertisement in *Blackpowder Hunting* magazine's summer 1998 issue, Gonic Arms touted its Magnum Muzzleloader as being able to produce a startling 3000 ft.-lbs. of energy at the muzzle and M.O.A. (1-inch group at 100 yards) accuracy right out of the box.

In the June 1996 issue of *Outdoor Life*, noted gun writer Jim Carmichael did an extensive test on in-line ballistics using four different scoped in-line .50-caliber rifles—the Knight Hawk MK-85, Remington Model 700 MLS, T/C Firehawk, and White Lightning, plus a Big Bore Express Alexander Henry Style Caplock rifle—shooting three-shot groups at 100 yards using 11 different bullets and a 90-grain equivalent charge of Pyrodex RS Select propellant—to test accuracy and muzzle velocity. Carmichael's tests showed what many of us have discovered doing similar range work—that you can achieve consistent 100-yard groups of less than 2 inches with the right bullet-and-charge combination from most quality production in-line rifles.

Both David Hale and Harold Knight use .50-caliber Knight DISC rifles for elk hunting. Why? "Because the use of a shotgun primer instead of an old-style percussion cap creates a no-fail 'fire in the hole,' " Hale says. "You know the rifle will go off under adverse weather conditions, and that's something you need, considering the fact that getting a shot at a mature bull is so difficult."

Knight likes to use sabot-encased conical bullets weighing between 250 and 300 grains, noting that both "penetrate like crazy even at longer ranges." He likes Pyrodex Pellets, using three 50-grain pellets in his DISC rifle. Where scopes are legal, Hale uses a straight 4× scope, but Knight prefers a low-power variable in the 2–7× class. If scopes are not legal, both Knight and Hale use fiber-optic open sights, which permit them to get a clearly defined sight picture in the lowest shooting light.

In addition to the usual "possibles" needed for muzzleloader hunting, both hunters are firm believers in using a laser range finder. "These tools don't make you shoot farther than you should, but help you confirm when you are inside the accurate range of your rifle," Knight says. "They're invaluable." Knight also likes to use shooting sticks, especially in brushy country where getting a clear sight picture sitting or prone is tough due to the height of the

The most popular and effective muzzleloader bullet style for elk hunting is the .50-caliber conical-type bullet weighing between 240 and 300 grains, encased in a plastic sabot.

brush. "Stoney Point Products makes excellent collapsible, light-weight shooting sticks," he says.

As far as shot placement goes, both Knight and Hale advocate shooting bulls right in the ribs, just behind the front shoulder, trying to take out both lungs. "Broadside and quartering-away are by far the best angles, especially at longer distances," Knight says. "Forget about Texas heart shots. They'll only result in a wounded bull."

A DEADLY HUNTING STRATEGY

David Hale's basic hunting strategy is simple, yet deadly. "I like to start out high on the mountain, and hunt the elk from the top down. This gives me the advantage of being able to easily see down into the thick timber when I am glassing, and makes it easier to hear bulls bugling. Also, there are few people in this world who can chase elk uphill. They're just too big, strong, and fast. If you can come in from above them, though, you have gravity working for you instead of against you. In the steep, rugged mountains of the West, this cannot be overemphasized."

This is an especially good strategy in the morning, because elk are generally working their way from low-level feeding areas up to higher-elevation bedding areas. "In the morning the thermal currents are also rising, meaning that if you can get ahead of and above the elk, you have solved the wind problem for the morning," Hale says. "Just as in whitetail hunting, defeating an elk's radarlike nose is paramount to success."

Hale also tries to pattern bulls. "If I find a bull moving his cows the same basic place two mornings in a row, the third morning I'll be ready in ambush at where I think they will be. That might be a specific saddle, bowl, basin, or a patch of isolated timber." Hale also notes that when hunting in New Mexico, Arizona, or other arid states, well-used water tanks or wallows can be dynamite stand locations during midday hours, especially in hot weather.

David Hale recommends climbing high before using your locator bugle during the early muzzleloader seasons. "You have to hunt the elk from the top down, or you'll never get into position for a shot."

A BASIC CALLING STRATEGY

Hale's key to muzzleloader success is seeking out bugling opportunities, so he prefers to hunt the earlier seasons. "I just like the warmer weather and longer days, in addition to the thrill of calling bulls to me."

"I like to use a big bugle call," Knight notes. "Our own Knight & Hale Big Bull, model 801, is a dominant bull bugle that we've used with great success. It's an esophagus hose with latex reed that's very easy to use. We use it to elicit a shock bugle. Once I get a bull to give me that first shock bugle, my bugle call goes back into my daypack, and I only use it again if he goes silent and I need to hear him as I try to get closer.

"We seldom, if ever, use the dominant bull bugle when we are within 400 yards of the elk. From the moment we get in close, we go to an excited cow-type call, using the Knight & Hale Magnum Estrus Cow Call, followed with a spike bugle call. This imitates a willing cow that has a subordinate bull tending her. If our target bull bugles back and is approaching us, I shut up instantly. He already has us pinpointed, and I let him do all the walking and talking from then on."

The Knight & Hale team also often employs a tandem tactic, where the caller sets up 60 to 80 yards behind the shooter. That way the bull, which is focused on the exact location of the caller, walks forward and into range of the shooter, who has set up in a concealed spot that permits a good field of fire. "When we do this, we try to stay within sight of each other so we can give hand signals," Hale says. "That way we both know what the other one is thinking and doing, and we can move if we have to as a team. That's the real key to the success of this type of setup."

A bull will often get in close but need a little more enticement to commit to the caller. When that happens, Knight likes to change

Using a modern laser range finder will help you know when you are outside your muzzle-loader's effective range. Both David Hale and Harold Knight carry a Bushnell Yardage Pro Compact 600, and use it constantly.

from the excited cow-type call to a softer, mewing-type cow call. "We use our bite-down reed call for this situation. When a bull hangs up, you want to get away from the excited sounds. You've already got him aroused with the excited estrus sound—that's why he came closer. Now, change it to a softer 'I'm over here, if you want me come and get me' sound. That is often the change that makes them snap and come in."

"You have to remain perfectly still when a bull is approaching the call," Hale emphasizes. "He's looking for movement, so anything out of the ordinary will spook him. You need to be hunting with your ears as well as your eyes. Listen for limbs crackling, rocks turning over—and have the gun ready. I like to set up at the base of a tree. That gives me a 'leg's eye' view of the approaching elk, and also lets me use the sitting position to shoot, which is very stable. If the bull hangs up and won't come into range, I may have to go to him. When that occurs I want to be on the same elevation as him, certainly not below, and I'm always checking the wind. The key is to not get in too big a hurry. He's answering because he believes you

Watching the wind is a critical part of all elk hunting, but especially when you are using a relatively short-range weapon like a muzzleloader.

are a cow. Don't spoil it by rushing in and letting him see you moving."

LOADING UP FOR ELK

While the classic patched round ball is still shot by some, where legal, smart muzzleloading elk hunters use conical bullets, most often those encased by a sabot. The sabot is a plastic wad, much like that found in a modern shot shell, that encases the bullet tightly in the barrel. This does three things. First, it prevents gas from escaping around the bullet, maximizing velocity. Second, it allows you to use a caliber bullet smaller than the bore size, meaning a lighter, and therefore faster, bullet. And third, it helps promote maximum accuracy. The military learned all this decades ago—one reason they use nothing but sabot-encased projectiles in tank cannons. Sabots also help prevent bore fouling by keeping the lead or copper of the bullet from touching the barrel, where it will leave hard-to-remove deposits. You'll also find them easier to load.

Many different companies offer quality muzzleloading bullets, including well-known blackpowder rifle makers such as Thompson/Center, CVA, Traditions, Knight Rifles, and Remington, as well as specialists like Buffalo Bullet Co., Muzzleload Magnum Products (MMP), Precision Rifle Bullets, Northern Precision, Parker Productions, Black Belt Bullets from Big Bore Express, and Game Buster Bullets. Well-known centerfire ammunition and bullet makers like Hornady, Barnes, Nosler, Swift Bullet Co., and Lyman also offer premium muzzleloading bullets.

There are two basic propellant types: old-style blackpowder and Hodgdon's Pyrodex, available in both traditional granulated and Pyrodex Pellets forms. Blackpowder—Goex and Elephant Black Powder are the most popular—is more susceptible to problems with moisture, although many hunters like it because it provides uniform velocities and accuracy. Pyrodex is less susceptible to moisture troubles (although you have to keep it dry, too, or it will not ignite), and it isn't quite as corrosive. The pellet form features preformed and premeasured charges that make loading quick and easy in the field. They work great.

Blackpowder rifles must be meticulously cleaned after each shooting session to avoid rust and corrosion. Cleaning supplies such as ramrods and attachments, patches, and cleaning solvents are often packaged in kit form, or they can be bought separately. These and other items like powder measures, powder flasks, speed loaders, percussion caps, cappers, possible bags and pouches, and other accessories are offered by many major gun makers but also by well-known aftermarket accessory manufacturers like Uncle Mike's and Bridgers Best. One excellent accessory item is the Dry Fire Breech Protector, a simply designed product that keeps moisture out of the breech area of many models of in-line muzzleloaders. Another is the Traditions EZ Unloader, which uses a blast of compressed air at the breech end to push powder and projectile down and out the barrel when unloading at day's end.

11

PRESSURE-COOKER ELK

If there's one thing I've learned about elk hunting, it's that there are few secrets anymore. With the widespread use of the Internet, information about a "hot spot" can be broadcast around the world in seconds. Having so much available information means that hunters are also more sophisticated in their planning and research. Add this to the fact that there are more people—hunters and nonhunters—in the woods than ever, and everyone is moving elk around.

The proliferation of ATVs and four-wheel-drive vehicles further means that virtually every logging road open for motorized travel during hunting season is hunted hard. Even backcountry areas well away from roads are hunted by outfitters, private individuals with horses or pack llamas, and enterprising backpackers. And once the snow flies, which pushes even the toughest old bulls down from tough-to-access high-country hellholes and makes tracking elk a reality, everyone and his brother with an elk tag, or who *knows* someone with a tag in his pocket, is out there stirring them up.

What this all means is that there are a whole lot of elk out there that have become hunter-wise in a big way. They react to this influx of humanity in a predictable way: They run scared. It quickly becomes difficult to find them.

When that happens, you can do one of two things: give up and go home, or adapt to the conditions at hand. You can still take an elk when the pressure's on. To do so you'll have to modify your standard hunting tactics, try a few new tricks, and—how do I say this tactfully?—get a bit lucky. Here's a plan.

LOCATING PRESSURED ELK

A key component of any public land elk hunt should be the anticipation of hunter pressure. Will there be lots of other hunters, or just a few? Where will they likely be coming from? How will they be hunting? On foot, horse, ATV? When these other people move in, what will the elk do? Where will the elk go, and how will they get there?

Like deer, elk often do two things when hunting pressure increases. One, they become increasingly nocturnal in their movements, doing the bulk of their feeding, watering, and traveling either on the cusp of daylight or after dark. And two, they head for the safest places within their range that they can find. These are usually the dark timber hellholes found at the bottoms of roadless vertical canyons and ravines, jungles of brush on steep hillsides, and the like.

To find the elk, you have to do what they do. That means glassing as early and as late as possible, and being willing to hunt the nasty stuff. You also have to be willing to try to find pockets of soli-

One of the keys to having a successful elk hunt in an area where there are lots of other hunters is anticipating what the other guy will do, and how his actions will move the elk. Climbing high and glassing as early and late as possible will put you in position to take advantage of pressured-semi-nocturnal elk.

tude, where other hunters either have not been, or haven't figured out yet.

SOLITUDE SOOTHES THEIR NERVES

Pockets of solitude, where elk may have moved to after being chased around by other hunters, are excellent places to fill a tag. That's because once elk find a pocket of solitude, where they are not bothered and where they can eat, drink, and rest in relative comfort, they tend to relax. They become elk again, not some hot-wired time bombs ready to explode. Sometimes it takes a little imagination to figure out where these pockets might be. Here are two examples:

Beginning with the August rut, elk migrate out of Yellowstone National Park onto national forest lands in southwestern Montana. Hunters know about this migration, and often line up near the park boundary line, anticipating new elk coming onto land open to hunting. Due to this hunting pressure over the years, however, the majority of the elk now travel after dark, slipping through this gauntlet unseen. They move along the spine of the mountain away from the park border several miles onto roadless areas, where access is tough for even the fittest of hunters. Once they reach this area, the elk calm down and begin acting normally again. Hunters who have figured out this pattern are able to slip into the country and hunt these elk without interference from those hunters who continue waiting for the few elk that do leave the park during legal shooting hours.

In many western states are large areas of high-elevation public lands that are fronted for miles by private ranches that refuse to allow the public access through their property. These public land tracts often hold good numbers of elk, especially after the shooting starts on nearby areas that are easily accessible by hunters. How can you gain access to these public hot spots? Two ways. The simplest, and most painful, is to walk into the national forest on obvious public trailheads, then pack the several miles into the mountains behind these ranches. The second involves researching public easements, which are access corridors sometimes found through private lands but are lightly publicized, if at all. The local forest service or BLM office may be able to point these out to you, but the surest place is the local county courthouse, where meticulous records of private property ownership and public land access are kept. Plat maps will show you exact borders, which you can transfer onto your own topographic maps. These are invaluable both for access pur-

Private land holdings in foothill country offer elk an ideal form of sanctuary in many parts of the West. Figure out how to access the far reaches of this posted land; hunting near the fenceline in hopes of catching elk as they leave croplands for timbered bedding ridges can pay big dividends.

poses and for keeping you from inadvertently trespassing on private land. You need to know this because you'll probably be hunting close to the property boundary. More than likely the elk will be feeding at least part of the time in the rancher's fields, then moving onto public timberlands to bed.

When there are lots of hunters afield, it gets tougher to fill your tag. Every year, though, a handful of enterprising sportsmen beat those odds and put elk meat in the freezer. Sometimes they just get lucky, but more often than not they make their own luck by hunting

When the pressure is on, hunting wilderness areas where access is difficult and hunting pressure is light can tip the odds in your favor. I shot this big 6×6 in Idaho's Selway-Bitterroot Wilderness Area from a camp 22 miles from the trailhead.

harder, hunting smarter, and looking for those precious little pockets of solitude where elk go to escape the hordes of fluorescent orange.

WHEN THE SNOW FLIES

Make no mistake about it: The epitome of elk hunting is the early fall, when the leaves are turning and frosty mountain meadows are ringing with the sounds of bugling bull elk. This is a magical time, and no one who longs to hunt elk should miss it.

Despite this, the bugling period, and the often dead time immediately following the rut, are not necessarily the best times to take a monster bull. In fact, they may not be the best times of year to take *any* elk, be it bull or cow. "Prime time" to harvest an elk is very late in the year, after the snows of winter have begun to fall, temperatures have dropped below freezing—or below zero—and the elk have begun moving down out of the high country into their winter range.

It is snow—and by that I mean serious, deep snow that stays until the following spring, and which can reach above an elk's belly line—that triggers the annual exodus of elk herds from the high mountains. In this the elk have no choice. They must leave to be able to find enough high-quality food to sustain them until the warmth of spring brings forth fresh new grasses.

When the snow flies, elk begin to move. This can be your best time to take a good bull, if you can also outwit the many other hunters thinking the same way.

This annual migration has a profound impact on elk herds. In some high-country areas, elk basically have two different home range territories—summer range and winter range. Summer range is much larger, and encompasses the high mountain meadows and steep timbered mountainsides. But when the snows come, elk are forced lower, to flatter ground where they can paw through the snow to find food. Generally speaking, winter range makes up 10 percent or less of an elk herd's yearly habitat. This smaller total habitat area will concentrate the elk, making them easier for you to locate.

Of course, in the warm regions of states such as Arizona and much of New Mexico, elk do not need to migrate from summer to winter range. In these states, the advantages of late-season hunts are fewer, as the elk can stay high virtually all year. But if you're hunting the northern elk ranges, try to do it during the winter migration.

One thing you'll find when you begin hunting those late-season snowstorms is that elk hunters turn out en masse for the same reason you're there: The elk are on the move, they're easier to find, and they're more vulnerable now than they were just a few days before. Smart hunters know they must strike while the iron is hot. However, many of these sportsmen have no clue how to hunt the snow, and end up wallowing around up to their armpits without a chance in the world of bagging a bull. Understanding how to hunt now is crucial to success.

MIGRATION HUNTS

When the snow-driven migration begins, bulls, cows, and calves begin appearing near roads, trailheads, and in ranchers' hay fields practically overnight. No longer does the hunter have to be half mountain man to reach the secluded high-altitude rough country that elk prefer during the general seasons.

That's not to say it's always a cakewalk. Usually you'll end up slogging through snow—often very deep snow—and fighting bitter temperatures and icy winds. But when the elk get closer to the roads, the hunting is always easier.

One problem in hunting the migration is that it can never be timed exactly, like the solstice or the return of the swallows to Capistrano. However, elk generally do follow the same historic routes year in and year out, and some elk will come down out of the high country about the same time each year. Without the deep snow, though, most elk—and almost all the bigger bulls—stay high until forced to come lower. In extremely mild winters, they may not migrate at all.

There is a direct correlation between the amount of snow needed to move elk and the distance they need to travel to reach their wintering grounds. If they have no more than a few miles to go, they are more likely to stay high longer. Elk that have to travel 40 or 50 miles—as many herds do—will depart the high country more quickly. As they move, they elk will cover many miles each day, often stopping for a few days in small pockets of habitat that have good forage. Again, the amount of snow is the driving force.

HOW TO HUNT IN DEEP SNOW

There are two basic ways to hunt in deep snow. The first is the standard spot-and-stalk technique. Climb high to a good vantage point before daylight, put on your warm clothes, and use your binoculars to spot elk as they travel or feed at first light. They often stay out later in the morning now than earlier in the fall, simply because they have to eat more to stay warm, a decided advantage for glassers.

If I don't find what I want this way, I do what I really like to do this time of year—pick up a fresh track in the snow and follow it.

This sounds simple, but usually ends in failure. Unless the snow is powdery quiet, the elk will hear you coming. The wind, which can help cover your sounds, must be steady to prevent elk from smelling you. Since the elk is walking and you have to follow

I have often spotted a herd of migrating elk in the evening from a road, watched it enter a spot in the timber, then climbed high in the dark and intercepted it at first light as the animals fed out into open meadows. You can do the same.

his tracks, you can't be too choosy about wind direction. Try climbing above the track, keeping it in sight as you follow, which will help you see down into the trees and brush and hopefully spot the animal more quickly. Always move slowly in the timber, using your binoculars to glass for pieces of standing or bedded elk. Of course, even if the track is very fresh, the elk may be miles ahead of you, and you'll never catch him.

Cow calling can be helpful when tracking elk in snow, especially if you bump some animals but they haven't smelled or seen you. Soft cow calling will often draw the herd back to you, giving you a chance to pick out a fat cow or bull to wear your tag.

WHERE TO HUNT

The biggest problem in hunting the migration is finding a place to hunt. At present, with the exception of Montana—in which the general rifle elk season runs through the end of November— most other elk states close their seasons before the snows come in strong enough to move the elk. Snow hunting is not unusual in British Columbia and Alberta, and Roosevelt elk hunters willing to brave the late season on Alaska's Afognak Island can also take advantage of snow-induced elk movements. Many states do offer special-draw tags for the late season, but they are extremely difficult to draw.

Prime areas to hunt during the migration are adjacent to national parks, where special late-season tags allow hunting for elk that are protected inside park boundaries but whose winter range is outside the park. Yellowstone and Canada's Banff national parks are prime examples. Finding exact migration corridors is as easy as asking a local game warden or game department biologist. These are not deep, dark secrets.

I've also spotted late-season elk right from a truck parked on a highway or paved county road, using a spotting scope and window

Fresh snow makes it possible to track elk without too much difficulty. While this can be a tough proposition, it can pay off big time.

mount to glass long distances into the mountains at first and last lights for both elk and elk tracks. I like to spot in the evenings. That way, if I see bulls I want to hunt, I find they'll usually be close to that same spot in the morning. In cases such as this I'll bite the bullet and leave camp many hours before sunup, trudging up the mountain in the deep snow, hoping to reach the area where I last saw those elk before first light. If things work out—and they have, many times—I spot the bulls as they feed in the same general area first thing in the morning.

Many a big bull is taken by hardy hunters willing to overcome the difficulties of hunting deep snow in bitter cold. In winter, when things are right, you will have the best chance you'll ever have of taking a monster bull. If that thought doesn't keep you warm, perhaps you should take up knitting.

12

RADICAL ELK STRATEGIES

I t had been the most frustrating, and yet the most glorious, week of elk hunting. The area I was hunting in southwestern Montana was simply crawling with elk. I was into bulls every day, sometimes several times a day, and yet on the sixth day I hadn't even drawn my bow.

Oh, half a dozen smaller bulls had come in, and I could have taken one had I chosen to do so. But I was after a good bull, one of those elk with many winters—and many hunting seasons—under his belt. I had called up a handful of big bulls so far, but each time they wouldn't come in close enough for a shot. They'd hang up in the brush 80 yards off and rake their horns, or stop and peek around a pine tree, or circle and try to get my wind. Lots of action, plenty of excitement, but nothing. Yet.

I decided to try something radical. Strapping half of a smallish five-point elk antler to my daypack, I went to an area where I'd seen a heavily antlered 5 × 5 bull two days earlier. At dawn I was in position, waiting for enough light so I could see my sight pins. When light finally came I bugled, and a bull responded instantly, not 100 yards down the canyon. I aggressively closed the gap, and we began a verbal sparring that heightened the excitement to a fevered pitch.

Thrashing and crashing, the bull came in, but like many of the others he hung up just out of range, on the opposite side of a small creek. I could see his antler tips above the brush as he raked and

When bulls hang up and won't commit to your calling, they sometimes need to see a piece of an elk to be convinced. Sometimes, showing them an antler (at left) can give them that confidence.

chuckled, showing off his muscle. It was the same big 5 × 5 I'd seen previously.

Taking my little five-point antler, I poked it above the brush pile I was set up next to, bellowed on my bugle, and pawed the ground with my boot, all the while twisting and turning my antler in imitation of a bull. I saw him raise his head, and when he saw my antler he was sold. He came rumbling down the creek bank like a tank, and as he plowed into the bottom I dropped my antler and readied the bow. As he charged up the other side he paused, looking for that pipsqueak five-point that had been there just a minute ago. My arrow centered his lungs. Thirty minutes later I was tying my tag to his main beam.

TODAY'S BULLS KNOW ALL THE TRICKS

Today's bull elk are smartening up. Mature bulls, those who have lived through more than four hunting seasons, have seen all the tricks. They've heard good and bad bugling, smelled the woodsmoke of camps large and small, seen the annual invasion of their mountain homes by hunters dressed in everything from total camouflage to pumpkin orange. They've been stalked, driven, chased, bushwhacked, and run around the mountain more than enough times to ever forget.

That's why today you need to be ready to give them something they haven't seen before. Not that textbook maneuvers won't work: They will. But nothing works all the time, and when the textbook answers the question "How much is 2 plus 2?" with "5," you know it's time to throw away the book and try something radical.

Merritt Pride is a longtime Montana guide and outfitter and one fine elk hunter. He also isn't afraid to try something different. Listen to this one.

"One time, I bugled a nice bull in for a bowhunting client who had a fancy bow with an overdraw and all that. When he went to draw, the arrow fell off the rest and hit the bow's riser—*clunk!*—and the bull trotted off," Merritt said. "The bulls in that area had been acting skittish all week, so instead of cow calling or bugling, I gave the alarm bark of a cow elk. Everyone says that when a bull hears this, he's gone. This bull came right back in.

"The hunter was so amazed that he let the arrow fall right off his rest again—*clunk!*—and the bull bolted off again," he said, grinning and shaking his head. "I couldn't believe it! But I barked one more time, and the bull stopped and came back, a little more cautiously this time, but he did come back. My hunter finally got it together and made the shot."

Then there was the time Merritt and I were hunting as a team. We had gotten a good bull going in a spot so brushy you could barely see your hand in front of your face. The bull had a small harem of cows with him, and they were above us on the side of a small timbered ridge across a creek cut. As the crow flies they were 75 yards off. As the hunter walks, they were 200 yards away.

The bull strutted back and forth across the face of that ridge, bellowing and ripping up brush. As he moved, we moved, staying parallel and not letting him get what he wanted—the wind. This went on for perhaps half an hour; then we heard some rocks clatter. He had had enough, and was going to take his cows over the ridge and away from this noisy madhouse. Merritt and I both realized what was happening the same instant, and when he looked at me with bug eyes and an expression that said, "Now what?", I whispered, "Let's charge 'em!"

So I did. As Merritt called and raked like a demon I crashed through the brush as fast as I could, right at the elk. Hopefully the herd would think the noise was that of another bull who was lathered up and ready to do battle. When I came out of the thick brush into a smallish clearing, there he was, not 40 yards off! He was a dandy six-point. Stunned that my charge had worked so well, I promptly stumbled over a fallen log. That broke the spell on the surprised bull, and he took off, fast! I would have had a good shot at him if I hadn't fallen.

THE TURKEY TROT

The "turkey trot" once worked to perfection for me and Drayton Martin, a guide for United States Outfitters. We were bowhunting the Gila Wilderness of New Mexico one hot, dry week, and while the elk were bugling, they weren't very active. One day, about 11:00 A.M., after we had chased a herd of elk up some very steep stuff and gotten busted by a swirling wind, we had lain down under the shade of a tall pine to rest our weary legs.

Suddenly, maybe 100 yards below us, we heard two bulls start squealing at each other. The wind was flat wrong, and we were just tired and mad enough that we decided to give them the turkey trot. Gathering our gear, Drayton and I started cow calling and chirping as we raced down the mountain toward the bulls. Before we knew it we had run smack into a group of cows, who scattered in all directions. We never did see a bull, but that was what, in our convoluted thinking, we had hoped for. "Just like fall turkey hunting," I told Drayton as we moved down the slope 50 yards to a nice, flat, brushy spot, set up, and began softly cow calling.

It took a little time, but 30 minutes later we both looked at each other knowingly. The unmistakable sound of a hoof striking a rock carried up the slope. We mewed softly and waited some more. We soon saw three cows working their way right toward us. The wind, which had been wrong, had turned with the afternoon thermals, and was rising right in our faces. This was beginning to get interesting. When I heard Drayton hiss under his breath, I knew we were in business. When I saw the thick beams of the 5×5 bull working his way toward the cows, my heart started to beat its way out of my chest.

The "Turkey Trot"—breaking up a herd of elk, then cow calling them back—is a desperation move, but can work. That's how this big bull fell to my arrow.

I'd like to tell you to look at that bull's picture on the next page. Fortunately for him, in my excitement I had forgotten to glass the shooting lane I had picked out. When he stepped into it not 35 steps away and I released, I knew he was mine. When the arrow made a 90-degree turn halfway to the bull, I was stunned. One little branch, the size of my middle finger, intercepted the shaft at the 20-yard mark with a crack like a Louisville Slugger hitting a hanging curveball. It took those elk less than half a minute to disappear forever.

The turkey trot is a desperation tactic, to be sure. I'd expect that most of the times you try it the elk will be so spooky that they'll take off running and won't stop until they reach the state line. But desperate times call for desperate measures. I'm sure I'll try it again someday.

ELK WANT TO SEE OTHER "ELK"

It seems that elk like to see other elk, or at least something with four feet that doesn't resemble a hunter. If they can't see another animal, they often get really cautious. But any little thing that gets them to believe that there really are other elk over there, and not some Bozo straight from the coffee shop in town, is often enough to win the day.

Take horses. I've had more than one bull elk bugle at the sound of my horses' hooves as we clompity-clomped down a trail. I can remember one rifle season in New Mexico when my partner and I were riding along through some rolling mountaintop meadows dotted with islands of heavy timber. Coming around the corner of one such timber stand, we ran smack into a herd of 30 elk, five of them nice five-point bulls. The textbook says stop, slowly turn the horses around, ride into the timber, dismount, and make a stalk on foot.

Not us. Instead we continued to ride right at the elk, who stood their ground trying to figure out just what in the world we were.

I've had more than one bull elk bugle at my horse's hooves. When bulls give themselves away like this, you must be ready to take advantage of them.

When we got to within 150 yards I turned my horse broadside, tossed the reins to my partner, who had moved his mount in between the elk and me, stepped off the saddle, sat down, and as the horses cleared my position, shot the largest bull in the bunch with my .338.

Textbook elk hunting? No way. Effective? You betcha.

TAKE TO THE TREES

An elk hunter's worst enemy, after his own clumsiness, is the wind. Bow season, rifle season, muzzleloader season, it doesn't matter—if you don't have the wind, you don't have a chance. How well do elk smell? Jack Wemple, an elk guide who took hunters into remote areas of Idaho and Montana for nearly 30 years before retiring after the 1999 season, has seen more big bull elk shot with a rifle on public land than anyone I know. Here's what he has to say.

"Elk can smell like few other animals you can hunt. Let me give you an example. I spotted a band of elk feeding along in an open meadow a half-mile from where I was standing. All at once I felt the wind switch, now going from me right to them. The second that breeze—and it was a gentle breeze, not a strong wind—got my scent to those elk, they threw their heads back, noses in the air for just an instant, then they bolted into the dark timber. At a half mile! How many elk do you think smell most hunters during the season and skedaddle before the hunters even knew they were in the neighborhood?"

Elk live in swirling wind country. Many longtime elk hunters—myself included—believe they purposely bed down during the day in areas where the wind always swirls as a means of extra protection from all predators. Textbook strategy says to stay out of these unstable wind areas so you won't spook the elk out of the country with your evil odor.

But when it's hot, dry, and the ground underfoot is as crunchy as crumpled-up newspaper, the elk don't move much during shooting light. If you want a bull, you have to go in after them. The way to avoid the swirling wind is to borrow a page from the whitetail hunter's textbook and get above it—in a tree stand.

Elk like to be near water holes and/or wallows in hot weather so they can stay cool and comfortable. Scout the mountain, and find a wallow or water hole that is peppered with fresh sign, usually tracks and droppings. Take a portable, backpackable tree stand and set it up in a nearby tree. Try to move in and set the stand up when the breeze seems to be blowing steadily in your face; once the stand is up, plan on spending the entire day there. Take lunch, a pee bottle, and a good paperback book to help fight boredom, strap yourself in with a safety belt, and be patient.

TAKE TO THE TREES. Elk don't like to move much during hot weather, so you have to turn the tables and go in after them. Take a portable stand and set up near a wallow or water hole with a lot of tracks and droppings. Try to move in and set up when the breeze is blowing in your face; once the stand is up, plan on spending the entire day there. You'll be surprised at what might come through a frequently used area such as this. Just make sure you have shooting lanes, and that you're ready to shoot, with gun or bow.

Give the stand a couple or three days if you have to. If you do, you'll be surprised at what you see from your perch. On a recent hunt into Idaho's Selway-Bitterroot Wilderness Area during the opening week of rifle season, a friend staked out a water hole under hot conditions for three days, and saw not only elk, but mule deer, whitetail deer, a coyote, a lone black bear, a mountain lion, plus numerous raptors, songbirds, and small game. He also shot a monster 6×6.

RATTLING FOR ELK

Another trick from the whitetail hunter's handbook is rattling. Hunting in New Mexico in 1990 with U.S. Outfitters and my good friend, guide Archie Nixon, reaffirmed my faith that rattling can be an effective elk technique that most people never consider.

I had shot a huge bull that scored 345 Pope & Young points with my bow two days earlier, and was now helping Archie guide another of his clients. One morning we looked down off a hillside and spotted a very large 6×6 bull stalking a lone cow. Suddenly another big 6×6 appeared; it was obvious what was going to happen next.

The bulls circled each other briefly, then locked horns in a for-real, someone's-going-to-get-hurt battle over that cow. They spun in a big circle, clacking their antlers, pawing the ground, and making a ruckus that would have frightened a dead man. As if by magic, out of the brush popped the head of another nice bull elk. Then out popped another. And another. And still another. In a matter of minutes five nice bulls came to the sounds of those bulls battling, together with a couple of cows. Why they came—curiosity, the breeding urge, whatever—who can say? But come they did—proving that the sounds of rattling antlers can draw a crowd.

Elk hunters have often raked and banged trees with limbs cut from other trees in attempts to mimic bulls raking antlers on brush.

This is fine, except that the sounds don't carry very far in the dense timber, or over uneven ground. The sounds of rattling a pair of deer antlers together carries much better, is realistic, and it works. Not all the time, just like horn rattling for deer doesn't work every time. But it's one more trick to pull out of your bag when the hunting's tough and textbook answers don't get the job done. I rattled in my first bull in Idaho's Selway-Bitterroot Wilderness Area back in 1981, and have done it several times since.

I'm not through experimenting with off-the-wall, radical elk strategies. For example, during a recent bow season I set up a tree stand near a wallow and erected an elk decoy. I figured that decoys have worked for me during whitetail season, so why not on elk? I have friends who use them with success, but as a go get-'em, chase-'em-down hunter at heart, I'd yet to give it a try. I used a life-sized

The use of decoys has become more popular, especially with bowhunters hunting areas where packing a decoy isn't prohibitive. This Mel Dutton Elk Decoy is lightweight and folds into a relatively small package.

Who says big bulls don't bugle after September? This old boy did in late October, answering a call and giving himself away. It can pay to break the rules and bugle after the rut.

McKenzie 3-D archery target as my decoy, sprayed a little commercial elk-in-heat scent around it, and bugled, then cow called, from my tree. Because I was hunting a limited-entry area of New Mexico famous for huge bulls, I chose not to shoot any of the nice 5 × 5 and smaller 6 × 6 bulls that came in that week. Two of them spooked at the sight of the decoy, but four bulls came in and checked it out long enough that I could have arrowed them had I chosen to do so.

When it comes to radical elk strategies, what will I try next? I'm not sure. Will it work? Who knows? One thing I do know is this: If the elk won't play by the rules, I'll throw out the textbook and play the game any way they like. When it comes to hunting today's educated bulls, it pays to get radical.

13

GUNS AND LOADS
(by Col. Craig
Boddington, USMCR)

Col. Craig Boddington, USMCR, is one of the most widely read and well-respected hunting writers of his generation. He is the former editor of Petersen's Hunting magazine, where he and I worked together for nine years. He has more worldwide big-game hunting experience than any other member of the outdoor writing fraternity, having made more than 50 African safaris, as well as innumerable hunts throughout the rest of the world, including all of North America.

Boddington is one of the finest field shots I've ever met, with any type of firearm. He's also a serious handloader, does technical gun testing, and is more qualified than anyone I know to speak from firsthand experience on rifles, cartridges, and their use on game.

Boddington is author of several excellent books on firearms and hunting, including Campfire and Game Trails—Hunting North

Col. Craig Boddington, USMCR, one of the country's foremost hunting writers and ballistics authorities, knows as much about "elk medicine" as any man in North America.

American Big Game; Shots at Big Game; *and his classic,* Safari Rifles. *For a list of his books and videos, or to order autographed copies, write him c/o Kodiak Communications, 7624 Whispering Trails Pl., Paso Robles, CA 93446.*

"I don't understand all this fuss about needing big guns for elk," a friend said. "After all, bowhunters take them all the time with just a dinky arrow."

True enough. Bowhunters harvest an amazing number of elk, as do blackpowder hunters and, for that matter, handgunners and hunters armed with .30–30s. So why do we read in all the magazines that elk rifles are nearly akin to Cape buffalo rifles?

First, let me say that I believe the American wapiti, pound for pound, is the toughest animal on the continent. He's big, to be sure, twice the size of a big deer and three to five times the size of most average deer. But more important than being big, he's strong and possessed of a powerful will to survive. He isn't as big as a moose, but he'll certainly travel much farther and much longer if hurt nonvitally.

I often hear that African game is much tougher than North American game. Whoever started that rumor didn't know much about elk. They're tough like Cape buffalo are tough, and if they had the same temperament, we wouldn't be discussing what kind of rifle is adequate—only the very largest would even be considered.

However, tough as they are, elk are not inherently dangerous. Hunters do put elk in the freezer with the full range of legal hunting armaments, from archery tackle to muzzleloaders to very light centerfire calibers. In spite of this, and in keeping with most writing about elk and elk rifles, I'm now going to say that the 6mms, .25s, and even the great .270s are not elk rifles. Nor is the time-honored .30–30. Here's why.

Elk are arguably North America's toughest big-game animal; you need a rifle chambered for a cartridge powerful enough to stop them. Boddington used an 8mm Rem. Mag. on this magnificent, big bull.

There is no question but that all the above-mentioned calibers, plus a whole bunch that are less powerful still, will cleanly take elk. So will arrows and a wide variety of projectiles from muzzleloaders and handguns. Lighter calibers, together with arrows, place severe limitations on the ranges at which shots can be taken, as well as on the angle of the shot that can be attempted. Some bowhunters enjoy this aspect of added challenge, while others merely accept it in order to spend more time afield. The point, however, is that bowhunters have fully accepted this limitation and its obligation. Although unusual levels of skill may increase range slightly, the ethical bowhunter knows that he must close to under 40 yards before shooting at an elk. And regardless of skill, he knows the animal must be broadside or slightly quartering away—no other angle will do.

In the same way, hunters carrying big-bore revolvers and muzzleloaders have accepted the limitations of their equipment; the range of feasible shots is slightly greater than with a bow, but in both cases, it's pretty much over with at 100 to 150 yards.

None of this is to imply that the average bowhunter, handgunner, or blackpowder hunter is a better or more ethical hunter than a rifleman. Some are, some aren't, and vice versa. Rather, their chosen arms have self-imposed limitations. Since they enjoy using these limited tools, they accept the restrictions. So long as legal caliber restrictions are adhered to, there's absolutely nothing wrong with riflemen limiting themselves by their choice of caliber—*so long as they understand that they have self-imposed limits and acceptable shots.*

Will the .30–30 cleanly take elk? You bet it will—but not at distances much past 100 yards. Its arcing trajectory makes exact shot placement too iffy, and without that perfect shot placement its bullets lack the energy to get in there and do the job.

Much the same could be said of cartridges such as the .243 and the various .25s, but for slightly different reasons. Flat-shooting lightweights like these do indeed allow precise shot placement at quite long range. But neither bullet weight nor energy is sufficient to ensure adequate penetration on any shot other than broadside behind-the-shoulder lung shots and the very risky brain and neck shots. Does this mean that these cartridges should not be carried into the elk woods? Not necessarily. Truly expert marksmen, comfortable with their light calibers, can indeed make them work miracles. This is especially true if they live in elk country. Hunters in such a fortunate position can wait for the proper opportunity to present itself—and, as should be obvious, it helps if the intent is to find any legal elk for the freezer, rather than a particularly big trophy bull.

In rifle hunting, bullet performance is everything. You must use thick-jacketed bullets that penetrate deeply before expansion on elk, like this 175-grain 7mm Speer Grand Slam (left) and 180-grain .30 caliber Nosler Partition (right).

Just like bowhunters, handgunners, and blackpowder shooters, hunters who insist on using inadequate rifles simply must accept the limitations of their equipment, know which shots can be attempted, and hold themselves within those limits. Some riflemen do get tremendous pleasure from using a particular rifle or a certain caliber, and so long as it's legal and the limitations are accepted, that's okay. But if the object is to get a nice elk—and especially if the hunter lives far from elk country and has a limited amount of time to hunt—then it seems to me that the sensible approach is to have the most adequate tool available for the job at hand. After all, if you're going to limit yourself by your choice of equipment, you might as well enjoy the seasonal advantage given to bowhunters and blackpowder shooters.

I suspect few hunters would try to make a case for the .30–30 or the .243 as adequate for elk. But what is adequate? Generations of campfire arguments have failed to answer this question adequately, so it's unlikely that this chapter will, either. But I will try.

Elk are big, strong, and tough. I once saw (not heard about, *saw!*) a bugling bull, full of adrenaline, take eight good hits from an 8mm Remington Magnum before he went down for good. Does that mean you need more gun? Of course not; the "Big Eight" is a fine elk cartridge. That was one of those anomalies, and I doubt the results would have differed if the bull had been shot with a .375 H&H or a .30–06—but it's an incident I'll never forget, and I keep it in mind whenever I select elk rifles and loads.

What's the upper limit of elk calibers? I'm not sure there is one, provided the shooter doesn't mind the recoil and the ranging capabilities are in keeping with the country. I've felt perfectly at home in elk country with a .375 H&H Magnum, and I know people who use .416s without apologizing for them. Obviously, rifles capable of dropping an elephant are hardly *necessary*—but you certainly can't say they won't do the job.

More difficult to define is the *lower* limit of sensible choices, and this is where arguments get heated. I said it before, and I'll say it now: the .270 is not an elk rifle. It's a great cartridge, a fine all-around performer, but it and its ballistic brethren aren't elk rifles, except in the hands of an expert hunter who's willing to wait for an optimum shooting situation.

The .270 will do the job when things are right, no question about it. And you can hedge your bets by picking your bullet with care, sticking with a dependable 150-grainer or, better still, a hand-loaded 160-grain slug or one of the semicustom high-performance bullets like the Winchester Fail Safe, Trophy Bonded Bearclaw, Swift A-Frame, or Bitterroot Bonded Core. But day in and day out, the .270 just isn't enough gun for the general range of modern elk hunting. It won't penetrate reliably on a bad-angle shot, and past 200 yards it lacks the energy I really want for elk-sized game.

How much energy is actually needed is impossible to define, and there is probably no exact figure since so much depends on shot

Here are three radically different approaches to elk rifles. The conventional Winchester Model 70 Super Grade (top) in .338 Win. Mag. will do the job anywhere. Synthetic-stocked Brown Precision in .375 H&H Mag. (center) is ideal for wet weather. The Winchester Model 94 Big Bore in .375 Win. is well-suited for short-range, thick-cover hunting.

placement, bullet construction, and even the mental state of the elk when it receives the bullet. Many years ago Col. Townsend Whelen theorized that you should have 1000 ft.-lbs. of energy *at the animal* for deer-sized game, and a minimum of 1500 ft.-lbs. for elk-sized game. If that's the case, then there are many cartridges that reach this minimum figure out to 100 yards. And still a great many more will do it out to 200 yards, including (with the right bullets) the .257 Roberts, .25–06, .264 Winchester Magnum, and a whole bunch more. The .270, for that matter, will deliver over 1500 ft.-lbs. at 300 yards, as will the .257 and .270 Weatherby Magnums. If I were a deer hunter with one of these cartridges and had purchased an elk tag "just in case," and if elk season were open and a bull jumped up, I wouldn't hesitate if the distance was moderate and the shot angle acceptable. I wouldn't *choose* one of these cartridges for an elk hunt, however.

All of the aforementioned cartridges achieve their impressive energies by pushing light bullets fast. And fast, light bullets are just what you *don't* want for large, heavy-boned game. Long, stable, relatively heavy-for-caliber bullets are what you want, and for my money the 160- or 165-grain 7mm (.284 caliber) is the minimum pill for elk.

Personally, I would prefer 2000 ft.-lbs. of energy at impact over 1500 ft.-lbs.—but if I had to choose, I'd take bullet weight over energy every day. We'll discuss the so-called close-cover, brush or timber rifles separately. First let's look at general-purpose elk cartridges, rifles you can take into elk camp anywhere with the assurance that your rig can handle any reasonable shot that comes along. As a personal choice, the 7mm Remington Magnum with a 175-grain bullet is the minimum I would choose for elk. However, if ranges are modest and the shooting is careful, I wouldn't argue with a .284 Winchester, .280 Remington, or even a 7×57 Mauser, provided good loads (almost certainly handloads) with heavy bullets were used.

The .30 calibers represent, to me, a big step up in performance. The .30–06 with a good 180-grain bullet is a fine elk setup, suitable for any elk hunting anywhere, and marginal only in very high alpine country where shots can run long. We'll take a quick look at the .300 magnums, but first it should also be said that, at moderate ranges, the lighter .30-caliber cartridges offer good potential for hunters who want to steer clear of recoil. Under 200 yards, there is nothing wrong with classics like the .300 Savage and .30–40 Krag with 180-grain bullets. And although, as a .30–06 fan, it galls me to admit it, the .308 Winchester will do about 95 percent of what the .30–06 will do—and do it in a lighter, more compact rifle.

The .300 magnums—.300 Winchester, H&H, and Weatherby, plus the .308 Norma Magnum—all offer a significant step up from .30–06 performance. The Winchester, H&H (with handloads), and Norma are pretty much equal, while the Weatherby beats them all

Col. Boddington (right) also guides elk hunters on occasion. Here he and his client pose with a Colorado bull, taken at 125 yards. The hunter used a Browning Stainless Stalker A-Bolt in .300 Win. Mag. loaded with 180-grain Winchester Fail-Safe bullets.

by a good margin. Within 200 yards, shot for shot, I doubt that any great difference could be seen on game between the .30–06 and any of the .300s. What the .300s offer is more reach—and they can give you that reach with heavier bullets. While the 180-grain bullet is nearly ideal for elk-sized game, the .300s really shine with 200-grain bullets. For long-range performance, there are very few combinations that can beat a well-constructed 200-grain spitzer from any of the .300 magnums.

The next step up is the 8mm Remington Magnum, a fine cartridge that just never really caught the public's fancy. Based on a necked-down .375 H&H Magnum case with the body taper removed, the 8mm Remington delivers nearly 4000 ft.-lbs. of muzzle energy with its 220-grain factory load, and shoots a good deal flatter than the .338 Winchester Magnum. If you have one, keep it and enjoy it. If you don't, I'm not sure it's a cartridge I could recommend although I like it a lot. To this day, more than 20 years after its introduction, it still suffers from a lack of good bullets. What this cartridge needed all along was a selection of good bullets in the 220- to 250-grain range. They're almost nonexistent, and with demand for the Big Eight dwindling instead of growing, I doubt a wide assortment of them will ever come along.

As good as the 8mm Remington Magnum is, hunters in search of something over .30 caliber are much better served by the .338 calibers. There are basically two, the .338 Winchester Magnum and .340 Weatherby Magnum. To this duo you can add the wildcat .338–06.

The .338 Winchester Magnum is one of Winchester's quartet of short magnums introduced in the late 1950s and early 1960s. It shares a shortened (to 2.5 inches) and blown-out .375 H&H Magnum case with the .264, .300, and .458 Winchester Magnums (and, for that matter, many other short magnums as well). I have written that the .338 Winchester Magnum would be my choice if I could

When choosing an elk rifle, select the most powerful cartridge you can shoot well, then pick tough, deep-penetrating bullets as your ammunition. This Remington Model 700 in .338 Win. Mag. fits the bill nicely.

have but one rifle to hunt North America with. I meant it. With 200- or 210-grain spitzer bullets, the .338 is flat-shooting enough for sheep, antelope, caribou, or whatever. With 250-grain bullets it will handle the largest bear. But mainly, with a 225- or 250-grain bullet, it is an *elk cartridge.* Jack Atcheson, Jr., a fine elk hunter, uses his battered .338 for just about everything. As he puts it, "Other cartridges put them down, but the .338 *numbs* 'em!"

The .338 starts its 250-grain bullet at nearly 4000 ft.-lbs. of energy—and at 400 yards it's still over 1500 ft.-lbs., with the bullet weight to back it up. It is not, in truth, as flat-shooting as the .300s, but it is certainly flat-shooting enough over any sensible ranges.

I certainly don't recommend marginal shots on elk or any other game animal. However, a long-dreamed-of elk hunt can come down to just one opportunity. It can be close, or it can be far; it can be in the timber or out in the open; the elk may be standing any way he chooses to stand. If you do your job, the .338 will handle any remotely reasonable shot. A lesser caliber may not.

If the .338 has one flaw, it's recoil. It hits hard and fast, especially with heavy bullets. And the .340 Weatherby Magnum hits still harder and faster. Not everyone can handle the .338, and fewer still can handle the .340 Weatherby. For those who can, this is another elk rifle without peer. All that was said about the .338 applies to the .340, except more so. It actually does shoot just about as flat as the .300 magnums, plus it delivers a great deal more in bullet weight, bullet frontal area, and raw energy. I have one of each, a .340 Weatherby and a .338. The .338 is more pleasant to shoot, but as an elk rifle I'm not sure which one I prefer.

The .338–06 is a wildcat based on the .30–06 cartridge necked-up to accept .338 bullets. It's obviously a handloader's tool, but with carefully worked-up loads using bullets between 200 and 225 grains, it actually doesn't lag far behind the .338 Winchester Magnum. In other words, it is to the .338 what the .30–06 is to the .300 magnums; up to 200 yards and a bit more the .338–06 will do everything its big brother magnums will do. It has the punch but not the reach. The tradeoff is that it does its work with surprisingly little recoil and muzzle blast, and can thus be built into a nice, light rifle.

The next step up is the .35s, and there have been a whole bunch that didn't quite make the grade. One that did is the old .35 Remington, but that's very much a short-range heavy-cover cartridge. That's the way folks think about the .358 Winchester, but with a good spitzer bullet the .358 will reach a fair distance beyond 200 yards, and it packs a lot of punch into that little case. It's one of the .35s that never quite made the big time, and that's unfortunate. Much the same can be said about the .356 Winchester, basically a rimmed version of the .358 designed for traditional lever-action rifles. It's a good cartridge, but it barely got off the ground.

The .350 Remington Magnum was designed to fit into Remington's slick little Model 600 carbine, and it was a real powerhouse in a small package. Remington has revived it somewhat in the compact, short-barreled Model Seven carbine, and a good thing that is. With proper bullets and loads, the .350 can reach up to 300 yards.

Perhaps oddly, the .350 Remington Magnum actually duplicates the performance of Remington's latest (and much more successful) .35 — the .35 Whelen. This 70-year-old wildcat created quite a stir when Remington legitimized it as a factory cartridge about 15 years ago. In fact, it created such a stir that there is now a wide range of outstanding .35-caliber component bullets available. Based on the .30–06 case, the Whelen obviously needs a .30–06 action, so it can't be put into a lever action rifle like the .358 Winchester or a short bolt-action rifle like the .350 Remington Magnum can. However, the Whelen is far and away the most useful of all the .35s. Accurate, light in recoil, and delivering an incredible punch, the .35 Whelen is a fine elk cartridge in all respects. With a good spitzer bullet of 225- or 250-grains, it will reach out to 300 yards with ease — and still deliver more than 1500 ft.-lbs. of energy at that range.

It should be said that heavy, large-caliber bullets traveling at modest velocities deliver a punch beyond what paper ballistics seem to indicate. Our "brush cartridges" certainly do, and my experience with the .35 Whelen on elk, moose, black bear, and wild boar places it in this category as well. I've had it do a fine job on elk, but one of the most spectacular things I've ever seen was a .35 Whelen literally upending a big Alaskan moose. I'm a believer in the caliber, and I love its soft rcoil and low muzzle blast. The only thing it won't do is reach out as far as the big belted magnums.

The .358 Norma Magnum, now experiencing a slight revival, will reach out as far. Its problem is the traditional .35-caliber dilemma — a lack of suitable bullets. Most of the new .35-caliber bullets are designed for Whelen velocities, and not all will stand up to the extra 300 feet per second that the big Norma offers. Still, it remains a fine cartridge for moose, elk, and big bears, and its Norma factory loadings are outstanding.

The last general-purpose cartridge we'll discuss is the .375 H&H Magnum. Without question larger and more powerful cartridges could be used, but there's really no reason to do so. And as much as I love the .375, there's really no reason to take one elk hunting—unless you *want* to. I've owned a .375 H&H most of my life and have always wanted to take one elk hunting, so I've shot quite a few bulls with one, including my first elk ever more than 30 years ago on Thanksgiving Day.

In truth, the .375 doesn't offer the flat trajectory of the 7mm, .300s, 8mm, .338, and .35-caliber magnums. But it obviously has plenty of power, and it has enough reach for most elk hunting. The traditional bullet weight for soft-skinned game is 270 grains, but if I were cooking up an elk load for the .375 I'd take a hard look at some lighter bullets, including Sierra's 250-grain boattail and the Speer 235-grain semispitzer. I'd also check out some of the newer limited-production "super premium" lightweight, aerodynamic .375 bullets. Jensen Bullets and Trophy Bonded Bullets, among others, make dandies.

The so-called brush cartridges are special-purpose rounds, only suitable for situations where you're darned sure a long-range shot won't be presented. Bugling hunts in thick timber come to mind, as does Roosevelt elk hunting in the rainforests of the Pacific Northwest. The timber cartridges—and the rifles that fire them—are made for fast action in close cover, and while they hit like a freight train up close, most lack both a flat trajectory and down-range energy for use much beyond 150 yards.

The .35 Remington is the most anemic of these cartridges, and indeed its paper ballistics—a 200-grain bullet at 2020 feet per second for 1812 ft.-lbs. of muzzle energy—are hardly impressive. Yet this cartridge has a fine reputation as a game-stopper.

Better by far is the .358 Winchester already discussed, and better yet is the cartridge the .358 replaced in Winchester's lineup—the .348 Winchester. Chambered only in the Winchester Model 71, and revived by Browning's limited run of Model 71 rifles, the .348 was and is an extremely powerful, hard-hitting cartridge. Its drawbacks are that the Model 71 is fairly heavy and poorly suited for scope mounting, but there's no argument about the job the .348 will do on elk.

Then come the heavyweights, the .444 Marlin and .45–70 Government. For close-in work both are devastating, but in the .444 it's important to stick with the 265-grain loading. The 240-grain load is a .44 Magnum pistol bullet, and will not penetrate nearly as well. A friend of mine in Colorado hunts elk in dense oak brush where

A quality scope is imperative on an elk rifle. Precise click adjustments, crystal-clear optics, and fogproof, waterproof construction are critical.

shots are always close, and his Marlin .444 has accounted for more than 20 elk. In the .45–70, some folks like the traditional 405-grain bullet, while others favor the faster 300-grain slugs. Both work, and neither has the trajectory for field shooting much beyond 100 yards.

In general, the important thing is to carry an accurate, dependable rifle that you shoot well and have confidence in. Bolt actions are the most popular among elk hunters, but if your choice is a single-shot, lever action, semiauto, or pump action, so long as the caliber is adequate the action type matters little. More important is a high-quality, clear, rugged scope. Elk are not small animals, so a fixed $4 \times$ is adequate, and a good all-round choice. Low- to midrange variables, from $1.5–5 \times$ to $2–7 \times$, are perfectly fine, and there's nothing wrong with a $3–9 \times$ provided you keep the power ring at a lower setting. Keep in mind that elk are large creatures, and big scopes lead to big temptations.

A buddy and I were field-dressing a nice bull I'd shot right at timberline when a big herd of elk paraded over the skyline behind us. In that clear alpine air they looked much closer than they were, and even at that I reckoned they were more than 400 yards away. We could have gotten closer, and we even discussed a route. But my buddy was looking through a variable scope turned up to $12 \times$, and in that eyepiece those elk were right on top of him. He insisted he could make the shot, so he tried it. From where that bullet landed, 400 yards wasn't even close by half! Of course the elk were long gone right after the shot.

Here's the bottom line on elk rifles: Shoot the biggest gun you're comfortable with. If that's a .30–06, that's fine. If it's a .338, finer still. But understand that no cartridge or bullet makes up for poor hunting skills or poor shooting. You'll have to work for your shot, and when it comes you'll have to do your part. If you do, all of the cartridges we've discussed—and many we haven't—will do the job. But only if you can put the bullet in the right place.

GENERAL PURPOSE ELK CARTRIDGES
FACTORY LOAD COMPARISON

Cartridge	Bullet Weight (grains)	Muzzle Velocity (fps)	Muzzle Energy (ft.-lbs.)	Remaining Energy (ft.-lbs.) 200 (yards)	300	400
.270 Win.	150	3000	2995	2275	1975	1700
.280 Rem.	160	2800	2785	1960	1625	1340
7mm Rem. Mag.	175	2860	3180	2310	1960	1640
7mm Wby. Mag.	160	3050	3305	2085	1630	1255
7mm STW	160	3200	3640	2890	2570	2275
.308 Win.	180	2620	2745	2005	1700	1430
.30–06	180	2700	2914	2140	1819	1536
.300 Win. Mag.	180	2900	3549	2699	2340	2018
.300 Win. Mag.	200	2830	3560	2830	2520	2230
.300 Wby. Mag.	180	3300	4352	3280	2834	2438
.300 Wby. Mag.	200	2900	3735	2645	2200	1820
8mm Rem. Mag.	220	2830	3912	2688	2201	1787
.338 Win. Mag.	210	2830	3735	2655	2215	1835
.338 Win. Mag.	225	2780	3862	2816	2384	2005
.338 Win. Mag.	250	2660	3927	2837	2389	1999
.340 Wby. Mag.	250	3000	4995	3812	3311	2864
.35 Whelen	250	2400	3197	2230	1844	1515
.375 H&H Mag.	250	2760	3955	2790	2315	1905
.375 H&H Mag.	270	2690	4337	2812	2228	1747

14

FROM FIELD TO FREEZER

There's an old adage among hunters that says, "The fun's over when you pull the trigger." It is never truer than when elk hunting.

Elk hunting is hard work. But if you think it's been tough up until now, just wait until you shoot an elk in some tough country miles from the nearest road. Throw in some nasty weather, like a snowstorm, or maybe a little thunder, lightning, and freezing rain. Stir in a pinch of heavy brush and a steep mountain between you and civilization. For good measure, add just a dash of slippery trail—if there's any trail at all—and you begin to get the picture.

Getting your elk out of the backcountry and down to the butcher shop in prime condition is no fun. Every year hunters lose lots of meat to spoilage in the field or the trim of the butcher's knife because they were not prepared to handle the difficult task at hand. Don't let this happen to you.

If you have to backpack the meat off a mountain, bone it out first. You'll have to make multiple trips, so be sure that your pack loads are easily manageable.

PREPARATION IS THE KEY

The key is preparation. You have to be prepared to take care of your meat before the hunt begins. If you wait until you punch your tag, the task will be overwhelming.

If you're hunting with a guide or outfitter, the job is immeasurably easier. They'll be responsible for meat care as part of the hunt, though you'll be expected to pitch in and help with the basic field-dressing and butchering. They'll have either packhorses or mules, or in the case of some private ranch hunts, four-wheel-drive rigs that can be used to transport the carcass out of the woods.

I've used a 4×4 truck twice for elk, both times on private ranch hunts in New Mexico. After years of doing it the hard way, I have to tell you this is good work if you can get it! On a hunt on the Vermejo Park Ranch one year, we were actually able to back the truck up to the small hillside the elk had fallen on, and literally roll him into the truck's bed, whole! We drove that bull back to the

If you can load your elk into a truck, consider yourself the luckiest hunter on earth. It's happened to me twice, both while hunting on private ranches.

ranch's cattle butchering area, where we hoisted it up on a commercial block and tackle, weighed the animal, and butchered it just like a cow. It was a dream come true.

Most of the time, you're going to have to make arrangements for meat care and transport on your own. It can be an overwhelming job for the deer hunter who walks up on his first elk. I promise you, your first thoughts will be, "Look how big this sucker is!" A mature elk will weigh between 600 and 1000 pounds (some Roosevelt elk, like those on Alaska's Afognak Island, can weigh 1300 pounds, or as much as a small bull moose). Unless you're prepared, you'll have trouble just rolling the animal into position to gut him out.

BASIC MEAT CARE

"In order to make the best products from your wild game, we need to start with game that was well taken care of in the field," says Doug Drumm, proprietor of Indian Valley Meats in Indian, Alaska. Drumm, who grew up around a slaughterhouse in Michigan, has lived in Alaska nearly 30 years. His business processes between 275,000 and 300,000 pounds of meat each year.

"There are many theories as to how to take care of meat in the field," Drumm continues. "I use a proven method based on principles used in the meat processing industry. The aim of this method is to make life harder for bacteria and flies by creating a cool, high-acid environment to slow their growth, limiting their food sources by leeching out blood, and then making a protective glaze coating."

First and foremost, always carry basic meat care equipment in your daypack. This includes a razor-sharp hunting knife, whetstone, lightweight saw or small hatchet, and 50 feet of nylon parachute cord or quarter-inch cotton rope. Have five elk-sized meat sacks in camp. Don't get *el cheapo* lightweight cheesecloth-type bags; they'll rip and tear, and probably won't be big enough. Invest in good-quality cotton bags that can be washed and used more than once. Be sure to have at least one roll of fluorescent orange flagging tape. A flashlight or headlamp with spare batteries are also worth their weight in gold when you shoot an elk at dusk and have to butcher it in the dark.

FIELD DRESSING 101

After approaching your elk and making sure it's dead, don't get so excited that you forget to fill out your tag and license in accordance with state game laws. I have seen hunters cited by unsympathetic game wardens for this very reason, so punch your tag before proceeding.

Step one is to get the elk into position for gutting. This can be relatively easy or extremely difficult, depending on the terrain, the weather, how the bull came to rest, and whether or not you have any help.

On a hunt in Idaho's rugged Selway-Bitterroot Wilderness Area, outfitter Rick Wemple and I were faced with doing it the hard way. I had shot a young 5 × 5 bull during the last five minutes of the last day of the hunt. The weather had been hot and dry all week, but that all changed not long after I pulled the trigger of my .338. The skies clouded over, light rain turned to slushy snow, and the wind picked up. It got coal-mine dark in a hurry that night. The bull had fallen down a 45-degree slope that had been the sight of a major fire the year before. Everything was slippery ashes and burned-out tree stumps. The tan-colored bull was now a charcoal mess. So were we.

We slid down to where the elk had come to rest against one of those burned-out stumps. If it hadn't hit that stump, it would have rolled another half-mile downhill. As it was, we were going to have to get the meat up 400 yards of that slippery slope before we hit flat ground and the trail.

Our first task was to make sure the bull didn't roll any farther downhill. So we dug into our packs, pulled out the nylon parachute cord, and tied the elk's antlers to a well-anchored stump. That accomplished, we managed to roll the bull onto his side, then tied one of his hind legs up and out of the way. When we were sure the elk was secure, we went to work and gutted him out. Trying to get all this done, while trying to prevent the elk from rolling down the hill, keep the meat as clean as possible in that wet-ash nightmare, and keep ourselves from drowning and freezing to death was quite the chore. To an outside observer, I'm sure we looked like Laurel and Hardy. It was a long night.

Because mountain elk rarely, if ever, are shot on level ground, I usually tie the antlers to a tree or boulder before field-dressing them. Failure to do so can result in the carcass slipping and sliding down into a nasty place that will compound your meat care troubles. That happened to me once, and I don't ever want it to happen again.

Once you get your elk positioned and secured, it's time to remove the innards. Field dressing an elk is just like caring for a deer, but on a larger scale. Assuming you have the right tools—a sharp knife, meat sacks, lightweight saw or hatchet for cutting off the antlers—here's how to go about it.

To get started, position the elk on its back, and spread the rear legs. (Having a friend hold one of the legs is most helpful.) First make a deep circular cut around the anus. Next make an incision beginning at the rear of the testicles straight up the center of the belly to the sternum, taking care not to puncture the internal organs. I like to rip right on through the sternum to the throat, and your hatchet or pack saw is the ideal tool for this. Now use your knife

Step one in caring for a downed elk is to field dress, then quarter and skin the animal so that the meat will cool rapidly. Keep the meat as clean as you can during this process.

to cut through the windpipe and, working your way down the body cavity, use the knife to cut loose the internal organs. You'll have to cut the diaphragm—that thin, tough muscle that separates the heart/lung area from the digestive tract—out. Once loose, roll the innards out of the body cavity. Be sure to work the large intestine all the way loose from the anus, and take care not to puncture the bladder and get urine on the meat.

Unlike deer, however, just getting the insides out of an elk isn't enough. Because elk are so large and their hides so heavy, they must be quartered and skinned to ensure that the carcass will cool properly. The only exception I've ever made to this rule was a bull a friend of mine shot while we were hunting in southwestern Montana one Thanksgiving weekend. The air temperature was −25°F, and we basically propped the carcass open with a stick after gutting to let that frigid air do its work. We then skidded the ice-cold carcass out whole on the snow with a packhorse.

If your elk is lying on its side, skin that side facing upwards first, laying the hide out on the ground as you go. Then remove the hindquarter, front shoulder, and back strap, laying them carefully either on the removed hide or on some pine boughs which you've cut for that purpose, allowing as much air to circulate around the meat as possible. Take pains to keep hair and dirt off the meat. It will be a hassle, but worth it in terms of quality at the dinner table. Some people like to quarter their elk before skinning, hanging the quarters by rope in a tree to make that task a bit easier.

Once one side is done, roll the elk over and do the other side. I like to bone out and remove the neck in one piece; it makes a nice little 20- or 25-pound addition to your pack.

I work on my elk differently if I have to bone it out. Instead of quartering the animal, I bone out one side of the elk, then the other, leaving the bones all attached. Let your knife follow the major muscle groups, and it will all come out right in the end. If you're a back-pack hunter and know that you'll be boning out your carcass, a 6-inch folding fish filet knife will make this task much easier.

However you get the meat off the carcass, don't forget the two tenderloins, the filet mignon of elk, located just under the backbone on the inside and to the rear of the carcass. And don't forget the elk's "ivories," those ivory-looking teeth found in the upper jaw.

Once the elk is quartered or boned out and cooling, it's time to prepare the meat for the trip down the mountain. If you have pack-horses, the quarters are just the right size to fit snugly into pack boxes. The same is true if you can get a vehicle to the carcass. But if you have to do it the hard way—by backpack—boning the animal out is the only way to go.

In some areas, using an ATV can make hauling meat back to civilization relatively easy. Make sure to check local laws regarding ATV use before bringing one into your hunting area.

TREAT YOUR GAME BAGS

Doug Drumm advises treating your game bags with a citric acid blend. "While the flies may light on a bag treated with a citric acid solution, the citric acid burns them, and they won't hang around long. The citric acid also helps inhibit bacterial growth.

"To understand how this works, know that bacteria grows rapidly at a pH level of 7.0," Drumm says. "The pH contained in lemons or limes is about 2.35. By using a citric acid solution on the bag, the pH level drops dramatically, helping kill off bacteria." You can make your own citric acid solution by combining the juice of three lemons, one large bottle of lemon juice concentrate, and one small bottle of Tabasco sauce. Soak the game bags in this solution for 20 minutes to one hour, then let them air dry completely (not in your dryer!). Store them in Ziploc-type baggies.

The actual pH level of game fluctuates according to their activity level. For example, an excited animal that has run a long way after being shot will have a low blood sugar level, which causes the lactic acid in the muscles to be higher and the pH level to go up. This, in turn, gives the meat a darker color and stronger flavor. "That's why, in terms of top-notch table fare, a clean kill is so important," Drumm says.

AIR DRYING/STORING MEAT IN THE FIELD

After the meat temperature has been lowered, it's important to air-dry the meat. "The key is to hang the meat out of direct sunlight in the shade, where any breeze will gently blow across the carcass," Drumm notes. "Excess moisture can be squeegeed off the meat with your hands, or wiped away with clean paper or cloth towels.

"Once the excess moisture has been removed, spray the same lemon juice mixture mentioned above in a light coat over the entire carcass. This will create a highly acidic protective glaze over the meat while it is drying." Once the meat is dry, it can be placed in game bags and rehung.

THE FLY TRAP

During many early season hunts—especially bow hunts—hot weather and flies are a major problem on elk carcasses. Along with the preventative measures already discussed, build a small fly trap near where you've hung the carcass.

"All it takes to build a fly trap is a can of Golden Malprin—available at many feed and mill stores—and a black garbage bag," Drumm says. "Eight to 10 feet away from the meat, lay a couple of branches on the ground. Pile meat scraps on and around the branches. Pour the Golden Malprin on and around the scraps of meat. Cut a slit in the center of the garbage bag, then place it loosely over the pile.

"The sun will heat up the plastic, which in turns heats the meat. Flies are attracted to the whole mess, and crawl in through the slit in the plastic. The Golden Malprin kills the flies. When you're ready to leave the area, put the whole trap into a Ziploc-type bag, carry it from the field, and dispose of it properly."

WINTER MEAT CARE

When hunting in freezing temperatures, skin the animal as soon as possible, then cover the carcass with a tarp or sheet of plastic (a space blanket works, too) for 20 minutes to one hour, Drumm says. "If the meat's surface starts to freeze, cover the plastic-covered carcass with snow to insulate it so that freezing does not occur until rigor mortis sets in." Rigor mortis is the process whereby the muscle tissue starts to stiffen up, and may take several hours, depending on the size of the animal and ambient air temperature. "If the carcass freezes before rigor mortis sets in, the pH level will not drop down to around 5.3," Drumm explains. "Then your meat will not be tender and have a good flavor to it."

PACKING MEAT OUT

Before loading meat into a backpack, realistically assess your own physical capabilities. One boned-out elk hindquarter will weigh about as much as a sack of cement—approximately 90 pounds. Can you carry that cement sack up and down hills, over fallen logs, and through thick brush, all the way back to camp? If

Backpack hunters will find that an external-frame pack will make hauling out meat much easier than an internal-frame pack will.

not, trim it down. It's much better to make more trips with an easily manageable load than to try to do the job in fewer trips with a too-heavy pack. Carrying too much weight in the elk woods is just asking for a fall, a pulled muscle, or a strained lower back. And if that happens, how are you going to get your elk out? In my planning, I assume it will take me six trips for one good-sized bull elk, including antlers and hide. On the first six-point bull I ever shot, my first load back to camp three hours down the mountain consisted of the antlers, football-sized liver, softball-sized heart, back straps, and tenderloins. I figure that load weighed in the neighborhood of 75 pounds—a typical load.

Outfitter Merritt Pride uses the livestock scales at his ranch to weigh most of the bulls taken by his clients. He estimates that the meat from most bulls—skinned, quartered, with the bones in—weighs between 330 and 430 pounds. Backpacking this kind of load any distance will take one man more than a single day. On my first elk hunt, my partner and I both shot big bulls in basically the same spot on a steep mountainside in the Selway-Bitterroot Wilderness Area. We were younger and tougher back then, and it still took us five days to get all the meat, antlers, and hides down the mountain and back to camp.

The better way to do it, of course, is with a packhorse. Smart elk hunters contact a local horse packer before they go hunting, and make arrangements for them to come and get their meat out for a fee. Most packers will ask between $300 and $500 to do the job. I used to think this was a lot of money until I backpacked out a couple of bulls. Now I hand over the cash with a smile on my face.

Remember that it is your job to quarter the elk in the field, bag the meat, get it cooling, and keep it cold until the packer arrives with his horses. This may be several days. But if you do your job right and the weather's not overly hot, you can hang an elk in the woods for

Making arrangements with a horse packer to haul out your meat prior to your hunt sure makes the job easier. Expect this service to cost between $300 and $500 per elk.

many days without it spoiling. Before heading down the mountain to get the horses, make sure the meat has been well taken care of.

In all the excitement surrounding the harvest of an elk, never forget that the ultimate reason we're there is to get the meat from the field to the dinner table in prime condition. Elk meat is some of the finest you'll ever eat, lean, flavorful, and full of protein, vitamins, and minerals that will contribute to your health. Take your time as you quarter and/or bone out the carcass. Pick off loose strands of hair and small sticks. Carefully trim away any and all blood-shot meat. Hang the meat in the shade so that air can circulate all around it and cool it quickly. If the weather's hot, cool the meat at night, then insulate it during the day with a sleeping bag, space blankets, or even items of clothing.

The difference between a top-notch elk steak, tender and full of flavor, and a tough, flavorless piece of meat is how you handle the animal once it's down. The Golden Rule of meat care is simple: keep it clean, and cool it down. It may seem like a lot of work at the time, but in the long run you'll be glad you took the time to do it right.

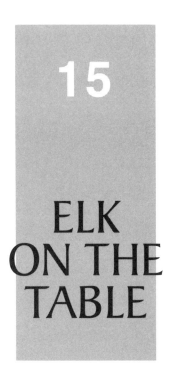

15

ELK
ON THE
TABLE

E lk is some of the most delicious meat you can serve at your table, bar none. It is also some of the most nutritious, and healthiest, meat you can eat.

A study conducted by Dr. Martin J. Marchello at North Dakota State University compared 8 different kinds of domestic meat with 18 kinds of game meat. The data compared energy, protein, fat, and cholesterol in each type of meat. All values were based on the contents of 100 grams of meat, or about 3.5 ounces. The table on page 202 compares various kinds of meat, and was compiled by the U.S. Department of Agriculture.

One finding in Dr. Marchello's study was that deer meat, both mule deer and whitetails, had a higher cholesterol content than

Elk meat is the finest meat you'll ever taste. All the work is always worth it in the long run. These hunters are enjoying the fruits of their labors.

beef. Whitetails had 116 milligrams of cholesterol per 100 grams of meat, and mule deer 107 milligrams per 100 grams, while most domestic meats, including beef, contained around 70 milligrams per 100 grams. Elk, on the other hand, contained 67 milligrams per 100 grams. When asked if this means that it is healthier to eat beef and other domestic meats instead of deer meat, Dr. Marchello clarified this point by saying that dietary cholesterol, or that which is absorbed by the body, is determined by the amount of fat present. There's little question that game meat is much leaner in that regard than domestic meats, and therefore better for you.

Subsequent studies conducted on the topic have shown that cholesterol levels in game meat vary, depending on several factors, including species, the specific muscle examined, the procedure for examining the meat, type of feed the animal has eaten, and whether the meat was raw or cooked. All studies have shown game meats—specifically elk and deer—to be lower in cholesterol, fat, and total calories than comparable cuts of domestic beef, pork, and lamb.

Dr. Ken Drew, a noted animal scientist from the Invermay Agricultural Research Centre in New Zealand, presented a paper entitled "Venison and Other Deer Products" at the International Biology of Deer Symposium at Mississippi State University in 1990. In that paper, Dr. Drew stated that "If science had been commissioned to produce a 'designer' red meat that had all the best attributes of our traditional farm animals and none of the perceived bad features, then the successful result would be something remarkably like venison." In 1990, an article in the *New England Journal of Medicine* recommended venison as a basic staple in preventative diets against such "diseases of civilization" as arteriosclerosis and cancer.

What it all boils down to is that diets built around game meats such as elk and venison instead of traditional fat-laced domestic meats like beef, pork, and lamb provide you with more protein, vitamins, and minerals, and fewer calories per ounce besides. Eating elk meat every week is not only fun and delicious, it's also good for you.

The accompanying nutrition value table illustrates just how healthy elk meat is. Given that, it's no wonder that more and more health-conscious sportsmen are carefully caring for their elk once it's down. Elk meat is very versatile, providing tasty meals as steaks or hamburgers, in stews and soups, as roasts, in casseroles, on the barbecue—any way you like it. Here, then, are a few of my favorite recipes for preparing elk. All are guaranteed to please the palate. *Bon appétit!*

HEALTH INFORMATION ON SELECT WILD AND DOMESTIC MEATS AND FISH
(all data based on a 3.5-ounce serving)

Type of Meat	Calories	Total Fat	Cholesterol	Saturated Fat
Elk	146	1.9 gm	73 mg	.7 gm
Deer	153	1.4 gm	89 mg	1.1 gm
Moose	134	.97 gm	78 mg	.3 gm
Bison	143	2.4 gm	82 mg	.59 gm
Lean Roast Beef	239	14.3 gm	87 mg	7.2 gm
Lean Ham	153	5.8 gm	58 mg	7.7 gm
Chicken w/o Skin	163	3.5 gm	85 mg	1.3 gm
Salmon	163	5.8 gm	87 mg	1.9 gm

FAVORITE ELK RECIPES

STEAKS

Basic Swiss Steak

2 lbs. round steak	¼ tsp. pepper
¾ c. flour	1 clove garlic, chopped
2 c. sliced onions	½ c. water
2 tbsp. margarine	1 c. chili sauce
2 tsp. salt	1 c. stewed tomatoes

Pound flour into steaks. Sauté onions in margarine. Remove onions, and brown steaks on both sides in leftover butter. Smother with onions, then add salt, pepper, garlic, water, chili sauce, and tomatoes. Cover tightly and cook over low flame until done.

Pepper Steak

2 lbs. round steak	½ c. cooking oil
1 sm. onion, chopped	3 tsp. lemon juice
2 tsp. thyme	2 tsp. meat tenderizer
1 tsp. margarine	½ c. whole peppercorns, coarsely
1 bay leaf	ground
1 c. burgundy	garlic powder to taste

Combine all ingredients in a mixing bowl, except meat, peppercorns, and meat tenderizer, and mix well. Place meat in plastic bowl, pour mixture over meat, and tightly cover overnight in refrigerator. Drain off marinade, but save it on the side. Pound pepper and meat tenderizer into steaks. Grill over hot coals, or broil in the oven, frequently basting with marinade mixture. Serve piping hot.

Chicken Fried Steak

2 lbs. elk steaks	½ tsp. onion powder
¼ c. flour	½ tsp. garlic powder
1 tsp. salt	1 tbsp. Worcestershire
½ tsp. pepper	½ c. cooking oil
3 eggs	½ c. nonfat milk

Slice steaks into serving-sized pieces, and pound until tender. Combine flour and spices in a small bowl. Beat eggs in small bowl; add milk, and whisk together. Coat meat pieces with egg mixture, then dredge through flour mixture. In a large skillet, heat cooking oil to hot. Fry meat in oil until brown on both sides, taking care not to overcook.

Butterfly Steaks

1 lb. backstrap steaks, cut 2 in. thick	¼ tsp. garlic powder
	¼ tsp. onion powder
½ c. flour	⅛ tsp. celery salt
¼ tsp. salt	⅛ tsp. paprika
¼ tsp. pepper	cooking oil as needed

Slice steaks down the middle, but not all the way through; they should resemble a butterfly when opened up. Mix flour and spices together in small bowl. Lay steaks on cutting board, dust heavily with flour mixture, and pound with mallet. Heat oil in skillet. Fry meat until done, taking care not to overcook.

ROASTS

Easy Roast and Vegetables

4 lb. rump roast	1 large green bell pepper
3 tbsp. margarine	1 pkg. onion soup mix
½ lb. potatoes	1 clove garlic
½ lb. carrots	¾ c. burgundy wine
½ lb. onion	2 tbsp. flour
6 celery stalks	salt, pepper to taste

Trim all fat from meat. Melt margarine in heavy skillet over medium flame. Brown meat on all sides. Remove meat from skillet, and place in large roasting pan. Peel carrots. Cut carrots, potatoes, celery, bell pepper, and onion into chunks, and add to pan. Peel garlic, slice thin, and add to pan. Add wine. Sprinkle with salt, pepper, and soup mix. Cover tightly, and roast at 350° for 2 to 3 hours, or until done to your taste. When done, remove meat and vegetables to serving platter. Blend flour into one cup broth, and bring to a boil. Cook, stirring constantly, until thick. Serve with sliced meat and vegetables.

Elk Roast and Cider

4 lb. elk roast	½ tsp. thyme
2 tbsp. cooking oil	1 tsp. rosemary
2 tsp. pepper	1 tsp. garlic powder
½ tsp. salt	1 tsp. onion powder
¼ cup flour	1 cup apple cider
1 tbsp. oregano	1 cup water

Trim away all fat from roast. Cut several 1-inch slits into meat, and rub thoroughly with oil. In mixing bowl, combine spices and flour, adding just enough water to make a thick paste. Rub paste into the meat, working it into the slits. Place in roasting pan filled with apple cider and water. Bake for 1 hour at 350°, constantly basting with juices. Cover, roast for 2 hours or until done to taste, basting every 15 minutes.

STEW MEAT

Elk Chili and Beans

4 lbs. stew meat, cut into 1-inch cubes	1½ tbsp. cumin
5 cloves garlic	1 tbsp. oregano
5 tbsp. chili powder	2 lg. cans sm. red beans
2½ tbsp. paprika	1 lg. can kidney beans
2½ tbsp. onion powder	1 large red onion
1 lg. can stewed tomatoes	cooking oil
	salt, pepper to taste

Peel garlic, and dice. Peel onion, and chop. Coat bottom of skillet with oil, get it hot, and brown the meat, sprinkling lightly with salt and pepper; drain. Rinse beans. Dump everything into 5-quart pot, including juice from tomatoes. Add water until it covers everything, stir it all together, and bring to a boil. Reduce heat, cover, and cook all day, stirring occasionally and adding water as necessary, ½ cup at a time.

Mountain Stew

3 lbs. stew meat, cubed	1 tbsp. cooking oil
2 red onions, diced	½ tbsp. garlic powder
4 stalks celery, diced	½ tbsp. onion powder
4 carrots, peeled and diced	1 tsp. oregano
1 bell pepper, diced	salt, pepper to taste
1 clove garlic, peeled and diced	dash of Tabasco sauce
4 medium potatoes, diced	2 tbsp. flour

In stew pot brown onion, celery, and bell pepper in oil. Add meat, spices, and continue cooking until meat is browned. Add 1 quart water and Tabasco sauce. Simmer for 1 hour. Add vegetables and simmer until they are tender (about an hour). Add remaining water. Mix flour with 4 tbsp. water until thickened, and add mixture slowly to stew; stir constantly as stew thickens.

GROUND MEAT

Basic Meat Loaf

1½ lb. ground meat	2 eggs, beaten
1 c. milk	1 tsp. salt
¾ c. dry bread crumbs	1 tsp. pepper
1 onion, diced	1 can tomato sauce

Briefly soak bread crumbs in milk. Mix all ingredients together in large mixing bowl. Mold into loaf pan and bake at 350° for one hour.

Pocket Hamburgers

2 lbs. ground meat	½ c. A-1 Sauce
1 yellow onion, sliced	salt, pepper to taste
sliced Swiss cheese	garlic powder to taste
sliced Tillamook cheese	onion rolls

In small bowl, mix meat, spices, A-1 Sauce together. Mold into thin hamburger patties. Lay slice of onion between two slices of cheese on top of one patty, then cover with another meat patty. Mold edges together, trapping cheese and onion inside. Cook slowly over open fire, making sure meat is done on inside. Serve on toasted onion rolls with your favorite condiments.

Stuffed Bell Peppers

1½ lb. ground elk	¼ tsp. pepper
½ c. cooked wild rice	¼ tsp. celery salt
2 tsp. garlic powder	2 large eggs, beaten
1 tsp. onion powder	6 large bell peppers
¼ tsp. salt	2 c. tomato sauce

In a large bowl, mix meat, rice, spices, and eggs together. Cut off the tops of the peppers, but save. Clean out peppers, carefully removing all seeds. Stuff meat mixture into peppers and replace the tops. Place in a Dutch oven and add tomato sauce. Cover and bring to a boil. Reduce heat and simmer for one hour. Add water if liquid gets low. Serve piping hot.

Spicy Ham Loaf

1 lb. ground elk	2 sm. cans chopped olives
1 lb. spicy bulk sausage	1½ c. bread crumbs
¾ lb. ham, finely diced	6 tbsp. brown sugar
3 eggs	salt, pepper to taste
1½ c. milk	½ tbsp. garlic powder
3 celery stalks, chopped	1 carrot, chopped

Combine eggs and milk. Add bread crumbs and spices. Add celery, carrot, 1 can olives. Mix well with all meats and pack firmly into greased loaf pan. Mix brown sugar with just enough water to form a thick paste. Spread on top of loaf, and top with remaining can of olives. Bake until done at 350° (about 1 hour). Let cool 15 minutes before slicing.

Pirozhki (Little Pies)

4 rounded c. flour	1 medium onion, diced
1 c. water	1 can mushrooms, diced
1 lb. margarine	salt, pepper to taste
2½ lbs. ground elk	2 hard-boiled eggs, diced

Cut margarine into flour as you would when making a pie crust. Mix in cold water with fork, and refrigerate overnight. Brown meat in frying pan, keeping it broken up into small pieces. Remove from pan. Cook onion, mushrooms in same pan until just tender. Add onion to meat, add chopped eggs, and season to taste. Shape one-fourth of dough into a roll about 1¾-inches in diameter. Cut into 1-inch slices and dip into flour. Prepare remaining dough in rolls, and use as needed. Roll dough slices into 3½-inch circles. Place a heaping teaspoon of meat in center of each dough circle; bring edges together, and pinch well. Place on ungreased cookie sheet, pinched edge down, and brush top with beaten egg. Bake at 425° for 25 minutes. Uncooked pirozhkis can be frozen, then thawed prior to baking.

Broiled Elkburger Loaf

1 loaf sourdough French bread	Parmesan cheese
margarine	1 tsp. salt
2 lbs. lean ground elk	1 tsp. pepper
1 tsp. Worcestershire	sliced onions

Split the bread lengthwise. Coat the cut surfaces generously with margarine. Combine ground meat with chopped onion, Worcestershire, and spices; mix well. Spread mixture liberally on two half-loaves of bread, building up the edges a bit. Place bread on cookie sheet 6 inches under the broiler and broil until meat is done. Sprinkle with cheese, and garnish with raw onion slices. Slice and serve.

16

THE FUTURE OF ELK HUNTING

Thirty to 40 years ago, deer hunting in the Rocky Mountains was at its peak. On the other hand, finding an elk to hunt was not that easy. Elk numbers were growing, true, but the most important big game animal in the region was the mule deer, of which there were plenty of does, young bucks, and older-age-class bucks with eye-popping antlers.

As we enter the 21st century, all that's changed. Today it is the mule deer that is in decline, being pushed out of its range by poor land management practices, high predation from cats and coyotes, and the proliferation of elk. What happened?

As the calendar turned its pages from the 1800s to the 1900s, western mountain ranges were almost solidly covered with old-growth forest. Settlers moving west from east of the Mississippi River

Proper management will ensure success scenes such as this well into the future.

never had a shortage of firewood and lumber. And while these forests were tailor-made for loggers, they were also mediocre habitat for supporting large numbers of big-game animals, whose overall population numbers were far greater in the more open foothills and grass-covered prairies.

During the first decade of the 20th century, several large wild-fires raged through these virgin forests. In 1910, a tornado of fire swept through the northern Rocky Mountains, and when it was through an area that had been a giant forest was reduced to a blackened landscape—much like large areas of Yellowstone National Park following the tremendous fires of the late 1980s. Within a few years, these burned areas became lush meadows filled with nutritious grasses and forbs. In little more than a decade, elk, deer, and bears had all moved in. Game populations began to soar.

While state records from the turn of the century are hard to come by, those that are available tell us that about 3000 elk were harvested in the year 1900. In 20 years that number had increased to around 20,000. The total western-states elk harvest peaked at around 140,000 animals in the 1960s.

After that, the top elk-producing states began experiencing slow declines in their overall elk numbers and, in turn, their harvests. Why? Three reasons stand out. First, the lush habitat created by fire 50 years earlier had begun returning to old-growth forests, habitat not suited to maximum ungulate production. Second, elk hunting regulations during those "heyday" years were much more liberal than they are today. Most states had rifle seasons that were open during the September rut. General elk seasons often stayed open until December, when snows pushed elk out of the high country into easily accessible winter range. And third, the growth of civilization continued, with new towns and cities, mines, dirt roads in the backcountry, and increased cattle and sheep grazing on public forest lands all encroaching into prime elk habitat. Elk numbers suffered greatly.

Fortunately, both state game departments and sport hunters recognized the need for improved elk management programs that included controlled burns and overall habitat management, more careful regulation of hunting seasons and bag limits, and a need to balance timber industry practices with wildlife habitat. Taken as a whole, the implementation of these practices has resulted in a comeback and, now, an explosion in elk herds across the West.

Thanks to transplants, elk have returned to areas east of the Mississippi River that they used to roam hundreds of years ago. Wisconsin and Kentucky have some elk today, for example, and anticipate having limited elk seasons in a few years. Michigan has been issuing 300 to 400 permits a year in recent years. Farther west, who'd

Elk hunting has a bright future across the West. Elk hunters spend huge dollars in communities large and small during elk season, and these towns roll out the red carpet for them.

have ever thought that states like Texas, Oklahoma, and the Dakotas would ever become elk hunting states? They have, and while tags are very limited, the hunting is excellent.

All this doesn't mean there are no problems in terms of elk management today, however. There are. Here are some of them.

- *Security Cover Loss:* When habitat is modified without concern for both game and nongame species—by logging, construction of housing, recreational developments like ski resorts, and golf courses—animals lose. For example, it has been shown that elk require fingers of thick cover in which to travel from place to place. Without this cover, they either refuse to make the trip or are so vulnerable to hunters they can be easily overharvested. Developments that do not consider their impact on summer/winter range migration corridors can destroy elk herds.

- *Backcountry Roads*: The largest impact that logging operations have on the long-term health of elk herds is not the cutting of trees, but the building of roads that open formerly wild, inaccessible areas to an influx of elk hunters. To combat this problem, many states are closing or restricting access on these roads during elk hunting seasons.

- *Predators*: With states rapidly enacting legislation—usually by the initiative process, not at the recommendation of game departments—that protects large predators, elk herds are increasingly falling prey to these hungry animals. The elimination of the trapping and poisoning of coyotes, and the full protection of mountain lions, or the elimination of the use of hounds in hunting them, have resulted in dramatic drops in elk calf numbers in some areas. Grizzly bear populations in Montana and Wyoming are booming to a point where Montana is considering de-listing grizzlies from the endangered species list and reinstating grizzly hunting for the first time in decades. Grizzlies eat a fair amount of fresh elk meat. And the reintroduction of the wolf to Yellowstone National Park and other federal lands throughout the West will certainly result in increased elk predation. Every elk a predator kills is an elk a hunter does not have an opportunity to put into his own freezer. These increased predator numbers are having a huge impact on western mule deer herds as well.

- *Ranchers vs. Elk*: One of the growing concerns in many western states is the problems that rapidly growing elk herds are having on the crops of lowland ranchers. In many areas the elk descend on crops like overgrown locusts in winter, eating everything in sight. Many ranchers, naturally, don't take kindly to this, and want every elk in the valley killed. And yet, many of these same ranchers refuse to permit hunters access to their lands to help solve the problem. States continue to try to balance the needs between landowners, hunters, and elk herds. It's a tough job.

- *Elk Herd Composition:* State game managers can closely control a specific elk herd's makeup—specifically the bull-to-cow ratio and the number of older, mature bulls in that herd. These same managers have just begun to survey hunters and the general public about what they want to see in their state's elk herds. Some hunters prefer lots of elk and the chance to harvest any bull or cow for their freezers. Others want a chance to shoot a trophy bull. Many states try to do both: have open areas where elk numbers remain high, but with harvest levels that reduce the chances of any bull living long enough to achieve trophy status, and limited-entry units, where harvests are closely monitored to permit many bulls to reach old age. Some states have imposed antler point restrictions to address the issue, too. To be a part of this process, elk hunters must continue to make their desires known to game departments.

- *The Antihunting Movement:* I've spent a lot of time in the trenches fighting antihunters over the years. I've learned several things about them. One, many are fanatical about their cause. For them there will never be any compromise, no middle ground. Another is that many of the officers of antihunting groups are in it for the fat salaries and perks they receive annually. They're nothing more than mercenaries, hired guns fighting as much for themselves as any cause. Also, most refuse to acknowledge the real way Mother Nature works, and don't want to know anything about the cruel way she can kill. Finally, these groups have no shame. They'll lie, cheat, and commit criminal acts in the name of their "cause."

This is my first bull, taken in the late 1970s in Idaho. It is my fondest hope that future generations will have the chance to hunt wild country that holds good numbers of elk and lots of big bulls, and share the same kinds of memories that I've been privileged to gather over the years.

The antihunters will not go away. Ever. All sportsmen must be willing to spend time and money fighting them on both local and national levels. Never give them any quarter or show them any mercy. Don't bother trying to compromise with them. They couldn't care less about your beliefs, needs, wants, and concerns. Get involved in the fight with your voice, your time, your dollars, and your votes. Write letters to newspapers, congressional representatives, the governor's office. If your children are being taught an antihunting agenda in school—and don't think it isn't happening across the country, because it is, more than you might think—visit the principal's office and school board. Don't only object to any antihunting literature used in the classroom; also volunteer to provide the school library with prohunting books. Support those prohunting organizations that support you and your beliefs. Unless we all become involved in the fight against the antihunting movement and educate the majority of Americans who are noncommittal on the issue of sport hunting, we will continually stand on the brink of defeat.

The future of elk hunting is bright. But like anything worth having, it doesn't come easily or cheaply. All of us who love elk, and elk hunting, need to become involved in the process. In so doing we will ensure that there will continue to be elk, elk hunting, and the magnificent country elk call home for our children's children to enjoy.

STATE-BY-STATE ELK HERD ESTIMATES

The following herd estimates were provided by individual state game departments prior to the 1999 hunting seasons. Remember that they are just that—estimates. We provide them here for general information only. Be sure to contact each individual state you're considering hunting before making any final plans.

State	Estimated Elk Population
Alaska	1500
Arizona	25,000
Arkansas	450
California	8000
Colorado	220,000
Idaho	118,000
Kentucky	170
Michigan	1000
Montana	100,000
Nevada	4250
New Mexico	58,000
North Dakota	700
Oklahoma	800
Oregon	130,000
Pennsylvania	350
South Dakota	4000
Texas	350
Utah	63,000
Washington	60,000
Wisconsin	50
Wyoming	110,000
Canada	
Alberta	26,000
British Columbia	43,000
Manitoba	8500
Saskatchewan	12,000

THE ROCKY MOUNTAIN ELK FOUNDATION

One of the biggest boosts ever for elk and elk hunting was the creation of the Rocky Mountain Elk Foundation (RMEF) in 1984. The dream of a handful of average, everyday elk hunters, RMEF has grown into one of the nation's largest conservation organizations, with chapters in all 50 states and around the world. The organization has raised untold millions of dollars to preserve and enhance elk habitat, works closely with state game departments on all man-

The Rocky Mountain Elk Foundation has raised millions of dollars for elk and elk habitat at fund raising events and auctions held all across the country.

ner of projects involving elk, and has frequently brought together hunters, ranchers, and government agencies, in never-ending efforts to help elk. It publishes both *Bugle*, a bimonthly magazine, and *Wild Outdoor World*, a bimonthly children's conservation education magazine.

For more information about becoming an RMEF member, contact the group at P.O. Box 8249, 2291 W. Broadway, Missoula, MT 59807; 1-800/CALLELK; on the Internet at www.rmef.org.

APPENDIX

Each fall, many nonresident hunters choose to hire a guide or outfitter to take them elk hunting. This simplifies the process greatly, eliminating the most difficult choice you have to make before the season, namely, exactly where are you going to hunt? The majority of elk hunters choose self-guided, on-their-own hunts with a handful of good friends. For this group of hardy sportsmen and women, deciding on where and when they'll be hunting is the game breaker. Pick the right spot, and you're in. Choose the wrong spot, and it's all over before the hunt ever begins.

To that end, the most important thing you can do to tip the odds in your favor is research potential hunting areas. This takes time and some creative thinking. Fortunately, today's hunters have more and better research tools at their fingertips than ever before.

This includes the Internet, where information on hunting abounds. In addition, many western states now make it possible to apply for both resident and nonresident hunting licenses and tags over the Internet or by telephone, with a credit card.

Because most states require nonresidents to apply for licenses and tags well before the season begins, it is important to begin your initial planning process immediately. I figure it takes me almost a full year to plan an elk hunt to an unfamiliar area, apply for and secure a license and tag, then get myself in shape and equipment in order. Following is a list of important planning contacts. Good hunting!

STATE GAME DEPARTMENTS

In addition to writing or calling individual game departments, you can also glean information from various states' Internet Web sites. They can be found at http://www.state.az.us (the "az" is for Arizona; substitute the two-letter abbreviation of the state you're interested in here).

Alaska Dept. of Fish & Game
P.O. Box 25526
Juneau, AK 99802
907/465-4112

Arizona Game & Fish Dept.
2221 W. Greenway Rd.
Phoenix, AZ 85023
602/942-3000

California Dept. of Fish & Game
1416 9th St.
Sacramento, CA 94244
916/227-2244

Colorado Division of Wildlife
6060 Broadway
Denver, CO 80216
303/291-7299

Idaho Dept. of Fish & Game
P.O. Box 25
Boise, ID 83707
208/334-3700

Montana Dept. of Fish, Wildlife & Parks
1420 E. Sixth
Helena, MT 59620
406/444-2535

Nevada Dept. of Wildlife
P.O. Box 10678
Reno, NV 89520
702/688-1500

New Mexico Game & Fish Dept.
State Capitol, Villagra Bldg.
Santa Fe, NM 87503
505/827-7911

North Dakota Game & Fish Dept.
100 N. Bismarck Expressway
Bismarck, ND 58501
701/328-6300

Oklahoma Dept. of Wildlife Conservation
1801 N. Lincoln
Oklahoma City, OK 73105
405/521-2739

Oregon Dept. of Fish & Wildlife
P.O. Box 59
Portland, OR 97207
503/872-5268

South Dakota Dept. of Game, Fish & Parks
523 E. Capitol
Pierre, SD 57501
605/773-3381

Utah Wildlife Division
1596 W. North Temple
Salt Lake City, UT 84116
801/538-4700

Washington Dept. of Wildlife
600 Capitol Way N.
Olympia, WA 98501
360/902-2200

Wyoming Game & Fish Dept.
5400 Bishop Blvd.
Cheyenne, WY 82206
307/777-4600

TOPOGRAPHICAL MAPS

As important as your weapon or a well-broken-in pair of hunting boots, topographical maps can be obtained from backpacking and camping stores and some larger hunting shops throughout the West. Maps can also be ordered from the U.S. Geological Survey, Distribution Branch, Federal Center, Denver, CO 80225; 303/236-5900. First call and ask for a state order map, off which specific individual maps can then be ordered.

DeLorme Mapping Company publishes the popular state-by-state Atlas & Gazetteer map books. These books have more than 100 pages of quadrangle maps that cover an entire state. They're great for beginning the planning and research phase of a hunt, as well as for navigating around the state once you get there. Their scale (1:150,000, or about 2½ miles per inch) isn't fine enough to permit using them to pinpoint potential hot spots or identify specific private property boundaries, but they are a constant companion in my office library and in my truck. Information on ordering volumes not available locally can be had from DeLorme Mapping Co., Two DeLorme Dr., P.O. Box 298, Yarmouth, ME 04096; 1-800/452-5931 or 207/865-4171.

NATIONAL FORESTS

The following regional headquarters of the U.S. Forest Service can provide a complete list of national forests within their region. From these regional forest headquarters offices you can obtain current information on logging operations, fires, and so on, as well as purchase specific national forest maps. The U.S. Forest Service, and its regional offices nationwide, can also be found on the Internet at www.fs.fed.us.

Region 1 (Montana, northern Idaho): 406/329-3089; 329-2411 fax

Region 2 (Colorado, part of Wyoming): 303/275-5350; 275-5366 fax

Region 3 (Arizona, New Mexico): 505/842-3076; 476-3300 fax

Region 4 (Nevada, southern Idaho, western Wyoming): 801/625-5262; 625-5240 fax

Region 5 (California): 415/705-1837; 705-1097 fax
Region 6 (Oregon, Washington): 503/808-2971; 326-5044 fax
Region 10 (Alaska): 907/586-8870

BUREAU OF LAND MANAGEMENT

Information on current land status, logging operations, fires, and so on, as well as maps of BLM lands, are available from these regional offices. Each state's BLM Internet Web site can be found at www.ak.blm.gov ("ak" is for Alaska; substitute the two-letter abbreviation of the state you're interested in here).

Alaska:	907/271-5960
Arizona:	602/417-9200
California:	916/978-4400
Colorado:	303/239-3600
Idaho:	208/373-3930
Montana:	406/255-2782
Nevada:	702/861-6400
New Mexico:	505/438-7400
Oregon, Washington:	503/952-6027
Utah:	801/539-4001
Washington:	(see Oregon)
Wyoming:	307/775-6256

STATE OUTFITTER ASSOCIATIONS

There are many excellent elk hunting guides and outfitters who will give you a great hunt for your hard-earned money. There are also a few fly-by-nights who will rip you off. Before any money changes hands, be sure any guide or outfitter you're considering is licensed and bonded by the state in which he wants to take you hunting. How to check up on this? Here's who to contact:

In Alaska (Division of Occupational Licensing), Arizona (Game & Fish Dept.), California (License & Revenue Branch), Nevada (Division of Wildlife, Law Enforcement Branch), New Mexico (Game & Fish Dept.), and North Dakota (Licensing Bureau, Game & Fish Dept.). Contact each agency at the address and telephone number listed earlier under "State Game Departments." Other state regulatory agencies are:

Colorado Dept. of Regulatory Agents, 1560 Broadway, #1340, Denver, CO 80202; 303/894-7778.

Idaho Outfitters & Guides Licensing Board, 1365 N. Orchard, Room 172, Boise, ID 83706; 208/327-7380.

Montana Board of Outfitters, 301 South Park, P.O. Box 200513, Helena, MT 59620; 406/444-3738.

Oregon State Marine Board, P.O. Box 14145, Salem, OR 97309; 503/378-8587.

South Dakota Professional Guides & Outfitters Association, P.O. Box 703, Pierre, SD 57501; 605/945-2928.

Washington Outfitters & Guides Association, 22845 NE 8, Ste. 331, Redmond, WA 98053; 509/962-4222.

Wyoming State Board of Outfitters and Professional Guides, 1750 Westland Rd., Ste. 166, Cheyenne, WY 82002; 307/777-5323.

Oklahoma and Utah do not have these types of organizations.

BOOKING AGENTS

Booking agents are really hunt brokers. They work on commission from the outfitters they represent. Using one does not cost you, the client, any more money than if you'd booked a hunt directly with the outfitter himself. Booking agents can also help mediate any problems that arise between clients and outfitters, sometimes offering discounts on future hunts if your dream hunt turns sour for reasons beyond your control. They want you to be happy so you'll book with them again. However, beware of fly-by-night booking agents. There are a million and one part-time booking agents out there, many of whom are in the business more for the fringe benefits than the success and satisfaction of the hunting public. One good source of quality booking agents is the American Association of Professional Hunting and Fishing Consultants (AAPHFC), whose member agents meet professional conduct criteria. More information and a members' list can be had by calling 717/652-4374.

INFORMATION, LICENSING SERVICES

Two excellent sources of information on all western hunting, and especially elk hunting, that you can use for a small fee are listed here. I've used both, and been very satisfied. They are:

Garth Carter's Hunter Services
P.O. Box 45
Minersville, UT 84752
435/386-1020; 386-1090 fax
www.huntinfool.com

Carter is a former Utah state game biologist and serious big-game hunter. His service publishes a monthly newsletter filled with information on the very best western hunts for all species, including elk. Also included are general state-by-state updates, updates on trophy units, drawing odds for the limited-entry hunts, harvest statistics, and more. Carter also helps members with nonresident applications, has information on private land hunting and ranch leases, and also works with a handful of top-notch outfitters as a booking agent. At $100/year, it's a great bargain.

United States Outfitters Professional Licensing Service
P.O. Box 4204
Taos, NM 87571
1-800/845-9929

George Taulman started the first western licensing service, where for a nominal fee his staff will do the research for you, then apply you for the best western hunts for whatever species you're interested in, including elk. If you don't draw the hunt you're dreaming of one year and choose to do so, Taulman will continue applying you for the same hunt year after year, helping you accumulate the bonus points you need to finally pick the tag. Taulman also offers top-quality guided hunting in several states; if you draw a tag using his licensing service, you are not obligated to hunt with his guides, but free to hunt on your own if you wish.

INDEX